Cosas

Folk Art Travels
in Mexico

Linda Grant Niemann

UNIVERSITY OF NEW MEXICO PRESS • ALBUQUERQUE

© 2018 by the University of New Mexico Press
All rights reserved. Published 2018
Printed in the United States of America
Library of Congress Cataloging-in-Publication Data
Names: Niemann, Linda, author.
Title: Cosas: Folk Art Travels in Mexico / Linda Grant Niemann.
Description: Albuquerque: University of New Mexico Press, 2018. |
Identifiers: LCCN 2017023892 (print) | LCCN 2017036343 (ebook) |
ISBN 9780826358769 (E-book) | ISBN 9780826358752 (pbk.: alk. paper)
Subjects: LCSH: Niemann, Linda—Travel—Mexico. | College teachers—Mexico—
Biography. | Americans—Mexico—Biography. | Mexico—Description and travel.
Classification: LCC F1216.5 (ebook) | LCC F1216.5 .N54 2018 (print) | DDC
917.204/835—dc23
LC record available at https://lccn.loc.gov/2017023892
The chapter "A Tale of Two Mexicos" was previously published as "A Tale of Two
Mexicos" in *Mexico, a Love Story: Women Write about the Mexican Experience*,
edited by Camille Cusumano (Berkeley, CA: Seal Press, 2006), 39–51.
Reprinted by permission.
Cover illustration: *Mermaid*, by Epifanio Fuentes
All photographs are by Valerie Dibble
Designed by Catherine Leonardo
Text set in Adobe Jenson Pro 11/15
Display is Adorn Bouquet
This is a work of nonfiction, but a few names and descriptions have been
changed to protect the privacy of the individuals.

For Leslie

Contents

CONTENTS

Illustrations

Acknowledgments

I would like to thank Kennesaw State University for a summer research grant and a Tenured Faculty Enhancement Leave, which gave me time to complete this project. I would also like to thank my colleagues Valerie Dibble for the photographs, Mark Patterson for the maps, and Pedro Javier Torres Hernández for guiding me in Oaxaca for so many years. My readers—Rosana Ayala, Donna Hunter, Carter Wilson, Pamela Hollway, Jennifer Butler, K. T. Maclay, Dorothy Mohr, and Susan Taylor—were indispensible. To my writing students who gave permission for excerpts from their work to be used here, thank you. Amy and Skye watched my house and cat while I traveled. And a thousand thanks to Helga Loebell, who offered me a writing sanctuary in San Cristóbal de las Casas.

Introduction

I grew up in a border state. Los Angeles, where I was raised, was about three hours from the border, but I went to college in Riverside, which was even closer. We used to cross the border to drink in Tijuana at the famous Long Bar. I can't remember how we got back to campus, but presumably we drove. My roommate at college crossed the border to have an abortion, which was illegal in the United States then. I remember the tension in the room when she and her boyfriend were getting ready to drive down there. She would have been about nineteen. I lived in San Diego for a year when my husband taught at the University of California in 1970 and then again four years later when I taught there briefly. We crossed the border to party. In a bar on New Year's Eve I saw two sailors tied together with a rope so they would stay safe. I drove my '56 Chevy across for a paint job and tuck and roll. I possess a photograph of me and Alain Cohan sitting on two zebra-painted donkeys. I am wearing a sombrero that says "Divorged."

When I left academia to work on the railroad, one of the first places I was sent was El Centro, California, and I crossed the border with fellow switchmen to drink. I later worked as a boomer following railroad work in many border or near-border towns: Tucson and Douglas in Arizona, Deming and Alamogordo in

New Mexico, and El Paso/Ciudad Juárez. In El Paso we switched out freight cars in yards that were bisected by the river and a chain link fence, often under the jeers of kids on the other side, who used the river culverts for water parks. We had the Border Patrol stop our trains a mile outside town, and hundreds of people would jump off the cars and run into the desert. Riders would hide under the floorboards in the engine toilet, in empty engines, anywhere and everywhere on the train.

The shadow border was ethnic and linguistic. The first language in El Paso was Spanish. Anglos, English speakers, were the most recent displacers, and they were struggling to maintain cultural dominance. As an Anglo, I was aware of understanding only a third of all conversations in my vicinity. It was here that I made a resolution to finish learning Spanish, a project that I had begun in high school but that was derailed by the prejudiced language requirements of my English major in college—German, French, Greek, or Latin. Kind of said it all right there.

No longer a drinker, I now crossed the border for gas, for shopping, for nightlife. I heard stories about the maquiladoras, finishing factories for US goods worked by legions of young Mexican women. A lot of my fellow workers went to strip bars and would denigrate the Mexican women who danced in them. Maids and yard workers crossed daily to take care of children, cook, and care for plants. Everyone would brag about how cheaply they had these services. And yet the brakeman threw water bottles off the engine to riders stranded on sidings in the desert. Seemingly adolescents, they lay under the cars to get some shade, and everyone respected the need for water. In the yard Anglos and Spanish speakers kept to themselves, carrying the shadow border with them. When I came back to El Paso to work after being gone for ten years, and having learned Spanish in the meantime, no one could believe it.

No Anglo brakeman the Chicanos knew had ever learned to speak Spanish.

"You mean you just learned Spanish?" one of them said to me. "Nobody does that."

I had a few work breaks from the railroad, and I started teaching part-time at the University of California Santa Cruz, filling in. I taught a section of a general course on Western civilization for Stevenson College; we read Miguel León-Portilla's Aztec account of the Spanish Conquest of Mexico, *The Broken Spears*, and a book on Aztec art. I had been to Mexico City early on with the Girl Scouts, a bus trip from Pasadena to Cuernavaca and back, and I had seen the center of Mesoamerica, to which the north connected but which remained underdeveloped. I started reading. About this time, I met Leslie Marmon Silko and reviewed her novel *Almanac of the Dead* for the *Women's Review of Books*. This monumental history of the Americas since the Conquest asks its reader to become educated. I took up the challenge. Learning Spanish was a part of this, but becoming as familiar with Mesoamerican old stories as I was with Greek old stories was a long process. I had to go beyond Spanish to Nahuatl, the language of the Aztecs. I learned about the names and aspects of the gods, the great attempted Spanish erasure of knowledge both written and spoken, and the incompleteness of that erasure. I learned about the ancient trade routes, south to north, the string of cities along these routes, the cultural interchanges that persist to this day. The Spanish were simply starlings that came to live in the nests already created, use the roads already established, and reinscribe the sacred sites already in use. The border, then, became a mark in the sand, so recent as to inspire contempt.

When I read Deborah Miranda's Bad Indians: A Tribal Memoir, I was reminded that California Native Americans had two borders cross their territories, one drawn by the Spanish, one by the Anglos. I saw the idea of border as a wave that engulfs cultures. I had no idea that Esselen was the name of a Native people. For me, Esalen was a hot tub retreat for California intellectuals who wanted to have sex and feel enriched at the same time. I was one of those people, of course.

When I started going to Mexico again in 1991, I went as a brakeman, continuing my restless travels as an itinerant worker following the rails south, investigating the language I had heard spoken in the Southwest, and becoming dazzled by the material folk culture. I started in the Maya world and then went to Oaxaca to learn Spanish, living with a Oaxacan family. After that I started to travel, by bus, outward in spokes from Mexico City and down to Guatemala. I would go to FONART stores (Fondo Nacional para el Fomento de las Artesanías, or the National Fund for the Development of Arts and Crafts), and then I would track down the crafts in their villages of origin. I would fly to Guatemala and then take buses across the border to visit friends I had made in Chiapas. Mexico was like my job as a brakeman, all about travel—travel hardship and reward.

Then I got what William Burroughs called "cancer at the door with a singing telegram." In seven months I went from working eight on, eight off as a switchman, climbing ladders and setting myriad hand brakes, to not being able to make my bed. While I was going through treatment, Mexico came to me in unexpected ways. The folk art of Mexico is heavily symbolic, referring back to cultural stories and ideas through design and color. My reading had taken me into the stories, such as the Maya creation of the world, and I let the redemptive power of the stories carry me through the ordeal of descent into the weakness of chemo and radiation treatment. I made a sand painting of my environment and sat in the middle of it.

Mexico was going through an upheaval of its own at this time: the Zapatista revolution in Chiapas, in 1994. I had left just weeks before it erupted. Right after my surgery, I went with Leslie to Chiapas to attend the second Zapatista convention. We saw 20,000 indigenous people marching in the streets. The people were filled with energy for change. Popular art took up the new images. Formerly barefoot women became military commanders. When I emerged from treatment seven months later, I was a recovering invalid coming back to a changed Mexico. First I went to Oaxaca to stay with my Mexican family. I got frequent infections, but the color and the art woke me up to life. I went to Chiapas to stay with my elderly friends and let them show me how to live.

When I went back to work on the railroad, I was a different person, physically and mentally. I had the brutal realization that I did not belong anymore. After struggling for a month at the job, I went to Mexico again, to postpone the inevitable. My experience of Mexico on that trip was one of incessant music, starting with a Saint Cecilia's Day three-tuba parade. I heard Armando Manzanero and Tania Libertad in concert in Mexico City. In Veracruz, I saw danzón, that hybrid of French country dance and African rhythm, performed in the city center.

I felt that I had to find a sanctuary within the railroad, because I had to work in order to heal completely. But when I went back to work, I had to admit failure. I couldn't work all night on the road anymore. I took a big cut in pay and had my seniority-based ability to transfer around restricted. I was stuck in a particular switching yard close to home that did not have a midnight shift, but it turned out this simple change was what I needed. I could sleep nights and get better.

My trips to Mexico continued to punctuate my life and act as mirrors. I noticed different things: I could understand where the migrants who worked in the railyards with me came from; I was on the same plane with them when they returned home to visit; I could speak their language. I started planning my exit from my job to return to the university as a teacher, while the railroad went through a crash and burn of its own—merger, dislocations, tension. I was following the path of my studies, since this particular road had run out for me.

Finally, I got a new job teaching creative writing in Georgia and left my old home to find a new one. One of the inducements was that they had a summer program in Oaxaca. Mexican color came with me in the objects that populated my new house. Georgia was also experiencing an immigration boom as workers came for the housing starts, the new residential construction projects. I began going to Mexico as a scholar, something that took getting used to. On a summer institute visit to Guatemala and Mexico, I remember feeling strange that I was no longer a free traveler. Now I had to have opinions and was traveling in a bubble of protection. Some wildness had disappeared. I also began taking students to Oaxaca to study Spanish in the summer. Now I was a guide, and they were the free barbarians. I thought of it as putting flip-flops on the ground. How else could they understand the migrants in their own neighborhoods? It was a small group at first, but over time I brought hundreds. I had a new role in Mexico. I brought money to middle-class host families. I could bring Mexican artists to visit the United States. I could teach American studies classes that looked at border issues and the relations of the southwestern United States to Middle America. I learned to dance danzón. Perhaps I will be so fortunate as to dance it as an old retired lady in Oaxaca.

Huipil, Oxchúc, Chiapas, 1994. Backstrap-loomed cotton, 30 × 36 in. Private collection.

A Tale of Two Mexicos

Cozumel, Quintana Roo, April 1991

MY DECISION TO learn Spanish started with a $200 round-trip fare that Veronica, my cop girlfriend, spotted in the Sunday paper. A romantic vacation at the beach was one of those things we had never done and probably wouldn't do, since, in retrospect, we were on the verge of breaking up. The big drawback, for her, was that she couldn't take her gun. For me, it was that she wanted to take her gun. I had no idea at the time that the trip would open a door into an unknown Mexico or that I would fall so in love with it that I would spend the next twenty-five years returning.

Veronica and I flew to Mexico City, our first stopover on our tour of the country. "Wow," Veronica said, "you can buy tear gas and Nicorette here." Her mood lifted noticeably.

In Veronica's view, the world was divided into actual criminals and potential criminals. It's not that I disagreed with this, but I had the luxury of distance. Unlike her, I could walk down a street in San Francisco without knowing that a slasher had ripped up two children in the apartment on the left. And I didn't have nightmares about trying to stop him. The slogan on her City of San

Francisco badge read, "*Oro en paz. Fierro en guerra.*" Gold in peace. Iron in war.

"It's Latin," she said. "They told us at the academy."

"*Pax,*" I said, "if it was Latin. *Paz* in Spanish." I could tell she was shocked, but after all, California was part of Mexico when the city was founded.

"Sometimes you look street smart and tough," Veronica would say, "but other times I look at you and think, 'Gosling.'"

Not understanding Spanish, in Mexico Veronica relied on her heightened senses to detect danger. Every stranger got a scrutinizing stare. It soon became clear we were not going to do much socializing on this vacation—but we would survive, that was the important thing. The beach at Chankanaab lagoon in Cozumel loosened us up. We put on snorkels and fins and bought chunks of bread to feed the fish while swimming. Although they looked peaceful from the shore, the fish—electric blue ones with brilliant yellow dots; queen angelfish; long, thin barracuda hanging around like dope dealers at a high school football game—attacked when bread appeared in the water. I felt fifty fish lips sucking on my bare skin, and I quickly let go of the bread and ducked. Resurfacing, I saw Veronica, terrified, shoot out of the water, a thrashing cloud of fish behind her.

"The bread," she managed, as I joined her under the *palapa.* "It was in my pocket, and they found it. Promise me you'll never tell anyone about this."

"I swear," I said.

"You know," she said, "a police horse is trained to lead you out of a crowd if you grab hold of its tail."

Before we left, Veronica read all the guidebooks, and we decided that we would rent a car and drive to the ruins at Chichén Itzá.

"Fine," I told her, "but you have to drive. I don't want to drive in Mexico."

No problem. She was butch. She would drive. After three days on the island of Cozumel, however, Veronica came down with the flu. She still wanted to see the ruins, so we decided to stick with the plan. But by doing so we were about to violate one of the two rules of travel in Mexico: only count on doing one thing per day, renting a car, for instance. The other rule is that time is flexible, but the rules aren't. When we disembarked from the Cozumel launch on the mainland, it was about 95 degrees, and since none of our luggage was on wheels, I ripped up parts of my suitcase and discarded them, along with half my clothes, to make my baggage lighter. We would be flying to Villahermosa from Canún after the trip to the ruins, so we needed to carry all our things with us. However, it turned out that car rentals were astronomically expensive in the nearest town—so we headed for Cancún on an hour-long bus ride. The local bus was actually a minibus. We crammed our packs under the seat and waited for thirty minutes while the bus filled up, which meant standing room only. Veronica had the aisle seat, which meant that she got to ride with someone's penis rubbing against her ear. Not her favorite thing, I could tell.

In Cancún, we managed to rent a diseased Volkswagen. Veronica had now come down with a sore throat, so I agreed, apparently not gallantly enough, to drive. I could have been more solicitous, I suppose, but I was busy keeping my death grip on the wheel. Every mile or so, we would hit an unmarked *tope*, or speed bump, which would knock us into the roof. Then small children holding items for sale would rush out in front of the car, forcing me to brake for them. I was also occupied with dodging head-on collisions with tourist buses that tried to pass each other on their way to and from the ruins. Terrorized, I'd decelerate and pull to the side of the road to watch the sleeping white faces pressed against the tinted glass as the air-conditioned bus passed within inches of us. At some point, it dawned on me that Veronica had ceased talking to me. No, not just because of her sore throat—now I was on the other end of that detective stare.

The hotel, the Hacienda Chichén, was a worthy journey's end, with flamboyant trees, cool verandas, manicured gardens, and guayabera-wearing Maya waiters bearing mango- hibiscus coolers in iced glasses. But it was all to no avail. We ate in silence, no doubt both wishing that the other women we were secretly dating were there instead. Unfortunately, frequently the trade-off for having a vacation with sex is having the Big Fight. And, after all, what more dramatic setting is there than the middle of the jungle?

"I should have known better," Veronica hissed, "than to go to the jungle with someone who doesn't care about me, one way or the other. Even when I'm sick."

"I care enough to show you ordinary courtesy," I snapped, the Pasadena priss showing through. "I care enough not to try to ruin your vacation."

But she was sick, and I was through driving, and so I apologized—repeatedly. And although she finally allowed me the excuse, it was clear that part of her just couldn't believe that I had been scared to drive.

I could practically hear her thinking, "Gosling."

The rift was patched for the time being. We were the first at the ruins the following day. Despite all the guidebooks and the scholarship explaining pre-Columbian life, I felt a geological rift. There was so much missing from the story. Veronica and I stood in the ruins of the ball court looking up at the impossibly high ring on the wall through which the heavy rubber sphere had to pass for score. "Kind of like having a relationship," I thought. "Equally impossible."

The next ruin on the schedule was Palenque, and to get there we flew from Cancún to Mérida, where we spent one night before flying to Villahermosa the next day. Since Villahermosa was a humid Gulf Coast oil town, we were off the tourist trail and had to rely on our wits. Our taxi driver pulled the "no change" routine on us at the bus station, and inasmuch as I was more or less speechless, he sped off with our two dollars.

"This place is a black hole," Veronica said as we quickly put our extra money in our socks.

At the station, I was totally focused on listening for the word "Palenque" over the static on the bus station's public address system. I was sitting next to a Maya couple, and so I tried asking them about the bus. They both laughed so hard that they almost fell off their plastic chairs, flashing gold teeth and clutching their sides. Then they pointed toward a door leading to the buses. All the departing vehicles bore destination signs. We found the bus marked "Palenque" and joined the other people waiting in line. It was hot. We were glad we had our purified water.

After waiting twenty minutes, a bus driver approached our bus. He wore black wing tips, navy slacks, and a thin belt with a Ray-Ban glasses case attached to it. He opened the door to the bus, and a little ripple went through the line, a shuffling of packages. But he ignored us all. The bus door closed behind him with a whoosh, its big glass fisheyes bubbling out in front of us. Cocooned and impervious, he bent forward slightly and combed his hair in the rearview mirror. He wiggled his mustache, extracted a tie from behind the seat, and tied it. Then, deliberately, he reached up and turned on a small personal fan and sat down in the driver's seat—all alone in his bus—for seven minutes.

Since at this time I was working as a passenger conductor on the railroad, and in spite of the sweat dripping down my nose, I had to admire his style.

In Palenque, we found the Maya Tulipanes, a bare-bones motel with working air conditioning. I loved the motel, actually, but Veronica found it lacking in the proper pizzazz for her last few days in Mexico. Since I was going to be going off on my own for two weeks to San Cristóbal de las Casas when Veronica returned to San Francisco, I agreed to move to the Mesón Palenque, a ritzy, hacienda-like hotel with a swimming pool, a jitney to the ruins, a Maya falconer, a gift shop, and a guard at the gate. Veronica told me that when she backpacked through India she would occasionally check into a hotel like this one to regain sanity before returning to the street, a reminder that she was an American and always had an exit card.

In its strange way, Mexico did not disappoint me in its surreal reminder that there is a special hell ready for those who have an exit card.

It became clear as soon as we tried to check into the Mesón Palenque that the desk staff was unaccustomed to foreign travelers on their own. The place was a hostelry for the tour-bus set, which usually arrived herded by a bilingual guide. It wasn't that I spoke no Spanish—I had managed to check us into the Maya Tulipanes, and I had managed to get us on a bus—but when I tried to put our passports in the hotel safe, we hit the language wall.

Leafing through the dictionary, I found *seguro*, which I thought meant "safe," and I asked for one. Reluctantly the desk clerk produced an envelope, which we signed and put our passports in. Now we needed change for a cab. Nobody at the front desk or the gift shop or the bar could cash the equivalent of ten dollars so we could take a cab out of the hotel. Finally, we refused to leave the desk until change appeared, and of course, then it did.

After a week, on our last day together in Mexico, we both had early morning buses and it seemed prudent to check out the night before. Where was our stuff in their seguro? The seguro, it turned out, was a safety deposit box with a key, and we couldn't have put our stuff in their seguro or else we would have a key, wouldn't we? I noticed that Veronica was about to erupt. It was just what she thought: we were surrounded by practicing criminals. At this point, another guest rushed up to the front desk, announcing that he had been robbed while taking a shower in his room. Veronica threw her wallet on the desk, flipped her badge out—which, thankfully, was in Spanish—and went into cop mode.

"Either our passports get here," she said, "or I call the police."

Miraculously, our manila envelope turned up.

Returning to our hotel room, Veronica set a chair in front of the door with a glass of water resting halfway off its seat.

"So we'll hear them in the night," she said and promptly fell asleep.

I wasn't so lucky. My thoughts kept taking a paranoid turn. The Mesón Palenque might not be a hotel, but a prison of some kind. I doubted they would let us leave in the morning. With these dark thoughts keeping me from sleep, I spent the night reading in the toilet and listening to the normal sounds of the hotel rustling and squeaking in the humid night.

We left at dawn like refugees, having been lightly breathed upon by an evil we did not understand. I kissed Veronica at the bus station as we set out in our different directions, in Mexico and in life, as it turned out.

Mexican buses are all named and decorated by the driver, and my bus was called *Escaleras del Cielo*, or Stairways to Heaven.

"Heaven would be a nice change," I thought. I took my window seat on the bus as it filled up with Maya on their way to the high country. The wall of jungle beside the road seemed impenetrable, yet as we climbed, people emerged from it and mounted the bus. The men carried machetes and plastic water bottles. The women had children wrapped in rebozos (Mexican shawls) and large bundles tied together with rope and carried with a tumpline. Fascinated, I realized that I was regaining my own point of view, that the suspicious nature of the world had vanished.

At a mountain town called Ocosingo, the Maya men getting on the bus wore handwoven white shorts and shirts, and the older men's legs looked like manzanita wood, twisted and muscular and dense as iron. I was the only gringa on the bus.

It was a Sunday morning, and as we descended into a valley, church was letting out in a town called Oxchúc. It was the first time I had ever seen an entire town in native dress—in this case, handwoven white cotton tunics decorated with broad, colored stripes. Because of the altitude and the bright sun, the white walls of the village, and the shadows of moving clouds, it was as if a flock of birds had suddenly flown by.

My friend Carter, a student on the Harvard Chiapas Project in the 1960s who wrote two novels about Chamulan life, had given me the names of two old friends in San Cristóbal. I was to meet them for lunch where I would be staying.

In San Cristóbal, I stayed in an upstairs room at Na Bolom, House of the Jaguar, the home, museum, and library of photographer Trudi Blom. Na Bolom was also a guesthouse and by now a San Cristóbal institution. Trudi and her husband, the archaeologist Frans Blom, had devoted their lives to researching, publicizing, and protecting the Lacandón rain forest and the unconquered Maya who lived there. Scholars and artists from all over the world came to use the library or live in residence. The Lacandón Maya were also welcome to stay whenever they made their way to town. Passing a Lacandón in the street was a ghostly experience. Wearing long hair and simple, sack-like tunics, they walked silently in a way that urban or even pueblo people couldn't. You got the feeling they could dematerialize if they wanted to. Trudi had sheltered them, visited them when the only way to get there was on horseback, and championed their fight. She was in her eighties, an institution herself.

But now Trudi was, in the spirit of the Day of the Dead, dancing with death. Her blue-lidded raptor eyes were raccooned with mascara. Huge glass rings dwarfed her fingers. During my stay, I would hear her after midnight wandering below me in her garden, accompanied by her vicious dog and entreating in a ghostly voice, "Vill nobody answer me?" Like a crocodile, she floated on the threshold between the worlds, waiting for silence or fresh blood.

In a room full of trekkers, she was dressed for a ball. We were all Pips to her Miss Havisham, and she held court at the head of the table when we sat gathered for lunch, alternately making pronouncements and abusing us. The two women her age who entered the room to join us for lunch on that first day seemed like Ariels in comparison. They too had a quality of body grown translucent, but their spirits were benign. They introduced themselves as Carter's friends, Marcey Jacobson and Janet Marren. Marcey was a photographer, and Janet was a painter, and they had been living together in San Cristóbal for forty-five years. Their Western clothes were clean and pressed, but well-worn and accented by Maya textiles. Their eyes were radiant, and they had strong opinions on politics and art. Their attention made everyone they talked with feel important. It struck me that I had not been in the company of such interesting and powerful women in a very long time.

After lunch they bundled me away in the back seat of their car, both of them excitedly turning around to look at me. The moment turned pink, as if someone had filled the car with bubbles; we had all fallen in love at exactly the same instant. Janet reached over the seat and gave my hand a conspiratorial squeeze, her artist's hands surprisingly strong.

"We're kidnapping you," she said.

I remember thinking, "I can't do this. They are eighty years old, and they live 4,000 miles away. How will I come to see them?" They lived only a few blocks from Na Bolom, and in a few minutes we were in their home overlooking the city. I tried to imagine what it would have been like to come here forty-five years before and stay. Marcey had told me that when they arrived there were only five cars in all of San Cristóbal.

As we sat in their living room, I told them about my life on the railroad, about Veronica, about my writing and what I had seen from the bus. They told me about their work and how they came to live there. Their community of artists, anthropologists, and revolutionaries was unique in Mexico, and I could see that it gave them this interaction between art and the community that was for them a rare gem. Janet's paintings were all over town. Marcey's photography shows attracted her subjects and their families. They also told me stories about Chiapas.

"Oh yes," Janet said, "we warned that tourist not to go hiking in the villages, but he was German, and he wanted to go out alone. Apparently, he touched a child."

"What happened?" I asked.

"They beheaded him," Janet said matter-of-factly. Then she added, philosophically, "The stranger the story about Chiapas, the more likely it is to be true."

It was so late when I left their house to return to Na Bolom that I took a stick of firewood with me to ward off the drunks who careened through the streets after midnight. I felt I had seen in Janet and Marcey's home a vision of what my life could be.

"Join us," Janet had said. "It is such an exciting time to be living in Mexico."

When I had left Veronica at the bus station, I wondered whether I would be lonely, wandering around San Cristóbal by myself, the way I often was on solo trips in the United States. Women don't often travel alone in the States, and connecting with the ones who do is hard. In our cars, hotels, and unsafe streets, strangers are wary of each other. In Chiapas I met solo female travelers everywhere. Weaving was the link. They were here to look at it and were willing to join up with others to travel to the weavers' villages. I had never seen anything like Chiapas Maya weaving. It was austere, intellectual, and transcendent. Done on a backstrap loom, the panels were parts of clothing, but if looked upon separately, they resembled paintings. It was immediately clear that they were also books. A woman's *huipil*, or blouse, or a man's *camisa*, or shirt, could be read for meaning, as well as for beauty. Meaning was embedded in all the daily textiles.

"How do you know what to weave?" I asked a woman in Tenejapa.

"I weave my dreams," she answered.

The Tenejapan weavers had one of the most organized cooperatives, with a storefront near the square and prices they considered fair for their work. The weavings—huipils, bags, sashes, and individual panels—had an ochre or maroon field with black designs and subtle color placement. They were fine art.

I was in the workrooms in the back of a church, where two women were hand spinning wool thread from the dyed skeins drying on racks, using a hand spindle and bowl to unravel the wool. They asked me and the woman I had met in town who wanted to see weaving to sit down and learn. They showed us the weavers' calluses they had on their fingers from resting the spindle there. I showed them the railroad calluses on my palms from gripping the handrails on the sides of railroad cars and the callus from playing the flute, where my flute rests between thumb and forefinger. I became aware of how much pride I had in the way that work had written itself onto my body.

As we rode the local bus back to San Cristóbal, I watched the driver's young son collect the fare, which had been my job on the San Francisco commuter trains. I realized that I was identifying with the way people worked here, much more than I ever did in the States.

You could say my work was archaic, but it was the way I had chosen to live: first in a cabin in the woods, heated by a wood stove, then dealing at flea markets, playing music in a street band, pumping gas, clerking in a liquor store, and finally working on both passenger and freight trains. After getting a PhD in literature, I had avoided as much as possible the world of offices and institutions. On my tourist card, I had checked the box for chauffeurs. I suppose most Mexicans did not see many working-class American tourists. My fellow railroaders were basically suspicious of travel across the border, as Veronica had been. They wanted to vacation with all of their expensive travel trailers and other recreational equipment, which often was stolen or broken into. They went to bars and got into fights. They were monolingual. They often resented the Mexican workers they encountered in the United States. They would never be here on this bus with a companion they had met hours ago in the town square.

A week later, on the plane home, I was aware that I was flying through much more than time zones. I knew I was going to learn Spanish fluently, no matter what. I knew I would someday live in Mexico and that it would be a welcome home. The plane was filled with Mexican Americans returning to the States from visiting their families. The border was just a line in the sand to them, and I had started to see it that way, too. There it was, below us, looking like a rail or a river, something to cross.

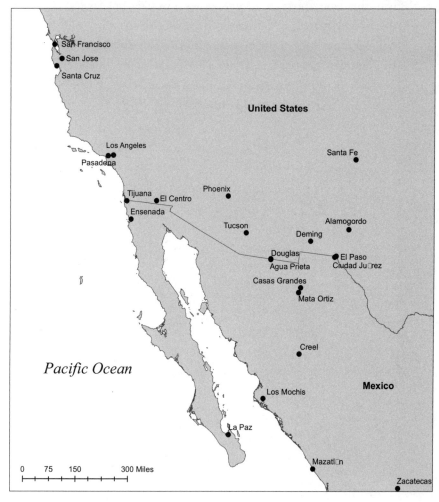

US Southwest and Northern Mexico, 2015. Map by Mark Patterson

CHAPTER TWO

Where I'm From

Pasadena, California, September 1946

I GREW UP in a house full of mothers: my sister, seven years older; my mother, thirty-eight when I was born; my father's mother, who lived with us; my mother's mother, who lived nearby. None of them worked outside the home. I lived in a net of protection that was so gossamer as to be invisible. My sister's cat was older than I was and lived to be eighteen. The furniture was never moved; the ruts in the beige carpet made by the legs of the dining table were eternal. The house was California Mission Revival style: white walls, viga beams, and red tile roof, in an orange grove block. Bougainvillea grew in the tiled patio. I lived outside, a sun-drenched physical existence. On Sundays we would drive down Rosemead Boulevard straight to Huntington Beach, where I learned to swim in the Pacific from my swimming teacher mother, who always took the chance to submerge. Spanish names were all around me, and a weekend occasion was Padua Hills, the foothills Mexican restaurant where waiters were emerging actors in a theater movement my parents knew nothing about.

My older sister played piano, and so when I fell in love with the guitar, I was sent instead to Donna Stinstrom, piano teacher, and then to a melancholy Hungarian who lived above a rattan-furniture store. The guitar, I was told, was not a real instrument. Besides, they already had the piano. I saved my money and bought a series of ukuleles, each larger than the next, until I saw, on an early trip to Tijuana, shops with walls hung with hundreds of guitars encased in huge plastic bags, smelling of wood and varnish, with gleaming tuning pegs—all the guitar wealth in the world, there, over the border.

I was by this time in a private school, Polytechnic—at considerable sacrifice. Here I could be looked down on for lack of a mansion, designer clothes, and a family Jaguar, but I had made a horse-loving friend whose mother owned a beat-up station wagon and horses in Mexico. Why my conservative parents allowed her to take us there, I can't imagine, but it was probably because my parents hadn't been closer to Mexico than Padua Hills. She would set up a tent on Estero Beach in Ensenada and drive through rural dirt roads to where her two bony horses were being boarded on a ranch. Then some muchacho would tie ropes through the horses' mouths, over their tongues and lower jaws, and Dorrie and I would climb up bareback, the animals' vertebrae sticking up inches above their meager flesh, and ride alone down irrigation ditches and paths back to the beach, where we would race the horses along the shoreline. There I learned *ropa* meant "clothes" and *hielo* meant "ice." And Mexico became the night sky.

My mother was a Girl Scout and later a Girl Scout leader, and so when the Girl Scouts organized a bus trip to their international center in Cuernavaca, Mexico, I was allowed to go—thirty-five teenaged girls and two leaders, a yellow school bus and 2,000 miles of travel. We ate mostly sandwiches made out of Pan Bimbo, Mexico's version of Wonder Bread, and drank Orange Crush. It was August, and the air temperature was the same as the water temperature in the beach towns along the Sea of Cortez. At Guaymas I walked out into the surf—and kept walking, the hot, briny water knee deep and the rippled sand forming ridges under my toes. At Mazatlán we stayed in a new high-rise facing the shore—one of the few at the time, but without air conditioning or a cross breeze. Perhaps this was my first inkling that there were uncomfortable places in the world where people lived anyway. I didn't see how. Discomfort was unimaginable. We remained enclosed within our yellow bubble as the bus progressed through Guadalajara, Morelia, and finally up the central plateau to Mexico City. The image that stays with me is of a wall of jungle beside the highway with children holding out iguanas to passing vehicles. When, thirty years later, I flew into Mexico City, I was looking in vain for that jungle, but it had all disappeared. A vast desert has taken its place.

In Mexico City I stayed at the apartment of a Mexican Girl Guide leader. At the time I didn't realize how unusual it was for a single woman to have her own apartment and work in the city. She showed me the thick wool sweaters she wore in the winter and made me *atole* for breakfast—a hot, thick, sweet, blond-corn drink that is a staple indigenous food. The sensation of tasting it has stayed with me my whole life, like my first taste of avocado, in Santa Fe, New Mexico, when I was thirteen.

I also went out on a date in Mexico City—with one of our Mexican Girl Guide leaders, her boyfriend, and her Cuban cousin, Pepe. We made the traditional paseo, or walk, around the Angel of Independence monument on Reforma Boulevard. During the paseo, it is possible to get out of sight of the chaperones for moments, and Pepe seized one of these to demonstrate French kissing, an act that seemed truly disgusting. Why would anyone want someone else's wet, slimy tongue in their mouth? I did, however, like trying to talk to Pepe and started the process of communicating over the language barrier through letters we exchanged after I got home to Pasadena.

This conversation became my ticket out of Polytechnic School. I needed a technicality. My social misery wasn't enough. But only Latin and French were taught at the school, and I argued that Spanish was necessary to live in our bilingual part of the country. On those grounds, my academic parents had to give way, and I found myself as a junior in public high school with a Spanish tutor coming to the house to help me catch up.

On a ski trip that year, I met Gay Georgi, a camp counselor who lived in a Mexican neighborhood and who took me to Olvera Street in downtown Los Angeles for scented candles and taquitos. I learned to dance from sneaking into clubs in Hollywood and watching the Mexican couples next to us. There was segregation, but also crossover. Old Pasadena looked Spanish, with manicured lawns. New Pasadena looked Mexican and was alive.

Unfortunately the health problems of my parents overshadowed everything those last years of high school, and when I arrived at the University of California, I was told that to study literature I needed to learn French and Latin or Greek. I therefore lost whatever Spanish I had and found myself speechless in French class and wandering in the Greek dictionary tracing verbs back through all their moods and tenses.

All of which was very unimportant when the educational system spat me out with an unsalable PhD and I found work as a railroad brakeman, following the craft throughout the Southwest. When was it that the desire to learn Spanish again began to reassert itself? No doubt the year I spent on the border in El Paso, understanding only half of the conversations around me and having the whole mysterious city of Júarez across the river, a closed book.

Juan Ugalde, my braking partner, would try to translate jokes for me. "Well, I say when a beautiful woman passes me, '*Chichocas con la puerta.*' It's kind of hard to translate. It's a play on '*Que chocas con la puerta,*' 'You might crash into the door,' and '*chichotas,*' which means 'big tits.' Another one is for '*Valgamedios,*' which means, 'Save me, God.' And I say, '*Nalgamedios,*' which means, 'Butt cheeks me, God.'"

The place names, all in Spanish, were only sounds for me: *Carrizozo*—"reedy," *Mesilla*—"side table," *Malpaís*—"badlands." The Texans didn't seem to feel this poverty of understanding and even took pride in being monolingual, pronouncing Spanish with the Texas twang, perhaps an accent developed against Spanish. "Hoe-la seenyora." How could it get much worse? I had arrived in El Paso in the summer of 1983, and when it turned cold in November, I went across the border and bought thick wool blankets to keep me warm. I now know these were Tarahumara/Rarámuri blankets, from the Copper Canyon in Chihuahua. I also bought Seri animals carved from ironwood and green obsidian paper knives and pyramids from Pachuca and Tarahumara tortilla baskets. I had no idea what I was looking at, but I knew that these objects brought places with them, carved and woven into them. And they decorated my bare room where I was sleeping on the floor and working freight trains around the clock northeast and northwest.

I had been back in California two years when I found myself at Price Club buying a State Department Spanish-language tape set for my commute from Santa Cruz to Oakland to catch Amtrak trains. Of course, I couldn't read the manual while driving, but I went through the tapes anyway, trying to reproduce the sounds at speed. Who cares, in the car, what you sound like? I shared the driving with Ron, my conductor, who had a strange reaction to the tapes. Whenever I would put one on, he would uncontrollably burst into song—presumably to defend himself from the mental challenge of listening, an insight into how threatening learning a foreign language is for North Americans. But then Ron had his own problems, apart from linguistic phobia.

I was singing also, the Mexican boleros, or ballads, along with the Trío Los Panchos. One of my earliest memories is of a song on the radio, "Allá en el Rancho Grande," which I used to pretend I knew the words to and sing along with, making up the sounds.

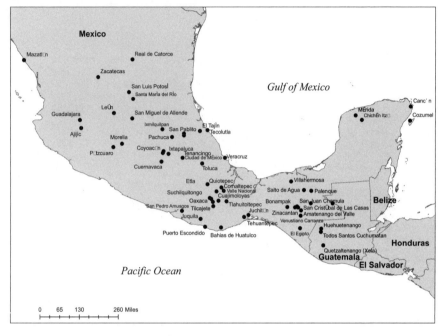

Mexico, 2015. Map by Mark Patterson.

Copper Canyon

Los Mochis, Sinaloa, November 1991

I TALKED MY girlfriend Celeste into going on a Mexican adventure. She was really cheap, and so she had figured out how tortuous a journey we could make by flying from Santa Cruz to San Diego, taking the Tijuana trolley across the border to the airport, and then flying from there to Los Mochis in order to catch the Copper Canyon train in the morning, thereby saving fifty dollars. My Spanish was a little better now, and I could count and order food, a skill that would get on her nerves in a few days, when she had had enough of being dependent. We got to Los Mochis, checked into a sleazy hotel where the walls didn't go all the way to the ceiling, and went out to look at the shop windows, seeing only imports, such as a rhinestone bustier, which Celeste admired. Since the streets were filled with jostling teenagers, we went to bed early to be ready for the train in the morning. The Chihuahua al Pacífico passenger train station at 5:00 a.m. was fog bound and full of middle-class tourists and backpackers. We took our seats, and the train started into the interior, climbing from sea level to the rim of the 6,000-foot canyon system. When we stopped at Bahuichivo, where vendors got on selling empanadas, or turnovers, and coffee, we appeared to be in Indian country. Around 10:00 a.m. we were climbing into a very steep sierra, over rivers bridged by the railroad.

When the conductor came around, I introduced myself as a railroader and showed him my railroad watch, the universal identifier. Conductors are big cheeses in Mexico. He shook my hand formally and invited us up to the engine, two Southern Pacific units, as it turned out. The engineer, the *maquinista*, had trained on the Southern Pacific simulator in West Colton, California, where I had worked as a switchman. We talked railroad. They had the same hours of service as we did, twelve hours maximum, and earned about $1,000 US a month. I made four times that, but we both felt underpaid. The cost of living in Mexico is less than in the United States, but not enough to make up for such a big pay differential. But then, laborers made $3 a day, and work in the maquiladoras paid about $10 a day. No, women didn't work my job in Mexico.

From the engine we could see the engineering feat of the trackage through the sierra, whose canyons, at 6,000 feet, were deeper than the Grand Canyon in Arizona and the second deepest on the continent, after Hells Canyon in Utah. The train traversed the famous ladder switchbacks, the bridge that looped over itself, and the railroad towns, now servicing lumber businesses, but formerly hauling out silver from the mines deep in the canyon. When we reached their crew change point, the station of San Rafael, we went back to the coaches. I thought it was odd that everyone in our car kept turning around in their seats and staring at us.

"They think you are Martina Navratilova," Celeste said. "I heard some people talking."

"Better than Elvis," I thought.

At Divisadero, right on the rim, the train stopped for tourists to take pictures with the local Rarámuri, who hiked up to the tracks with arrows and baskets, wearing long skirts and loose blouses. They lived in the canyon, raised cattle, and ran long distances up and down the perpendicular walls. Of course, I had seen their work in El Paso when I worked there in 1983 as a brakeman, but I had no idea where it came from. Their blankets had kept me warm. There was a fancy hotel, like El Tovar at the Grand Canyon, perched on the edge, the destination for the well-heeled tourists on the train. It seemed like a frozen moment from the early days of the Santa Fe railroad in the North American Southwest. We got off at Creel, a lumber town and the jumping-off point for trips down the canyon, and rolled our bags to a cheap and clean hotel, Casa Margarita's. Then we set out to explore the town. It was chilly up in the mountains, and Celeste hadn't brought warm clothes, and of course she wouldn't spend money on mittens in Creel. We booked a Suburban for a trip into the canyon the next day. There was a village down there called Batopilas that I was curious about. It had been a silver-mining boomtown before the revolution, and the Mexican American writer Victor Villaseñor told family stories about canyon bushmaster snakes so large they could knock a man off a horse.

Meanwhile, we found a rustic café with a piano bar, and Mexico warmed us. A local joined us at our table and actually said, "Spanish is the language of love." Back home, Celeste had often invited me over for dinner to seduce me, but I drew the line somewhere, not wanting to make nice with her husband while considering running off with his wife. It was Santa Cruz, though, and open marriages were the thing. My own open marriage had ended in a creative divorce years before.

As we were hiking with our new friend around Creel the next morning, I noticed someone running toward us in the distance.

As he got closer, I could see he was Rarámuri, wearing their loose shirt and triangular shorts. He passed us and kept running, soon out of sight. Celeste didn't seem impressed. She was busy talking. It was starting to dawn on me that not everyone would share my feeling for or even notice how amazing Mexico was.

At ten our Suburban showed up. We were going to try to get all the way down into the canyon, depending on conditions. It started to rain. On a dirt road it took about an hour to reach the rim, and then we started down the switchbacks. There was a public bus that made this trip in the early hours. I tried to imagine it fitting on this road and couldn't. The rear of the bus would have to overhang the turns. As it was, Celeste was white-knuckling it in the Suburban. Her view of Mexico had been that it was all beach. In fact, very little of Mexico is at sea level, and the colonial Spaniards couldn't get away from the coast fast enough. They built most of their principal cities above 5,000 feet, where altitude compensated for latitude.

Incredibly, we passed herds of goats clambering up the sheer rock face; they belonged to the Rarámuri, who lived in caves set into the canyon walls. A thin stream, green and polluted with engine oil bottles, cut into the cliffs. The cliff walls, dotted with cactus, were green also, unlike the Grand Canyon, to which Copper Canyon could be compared. Five finger rivers cut into this canyon system, like an open hand. When the French actor and poet Antonin Artaud came here in the 1930s, he had to be strapped on a horse, and he kept seeing allegorical signs on the rock walls. He went to see a peyote ceremony in Narárachi, a town still famous for peyote "raspers," or shamans. Amid the pissing and farting shamans, his peyote experience gave him insight into what he called the true nature of reality. The Rarámuri still remember his visit, my friend Leslie Marmon Silko told me. When she went to an indigenous writers' conference in Chihuahua City, the local writers were still recalling Artaud.

With the rain, the dirt road was getting difficult for even our four-wheel drive, and the driver stopped at a small store at La Bufa, a wide place in the road three-quarters of the way down. I went to use the toilet, and when I opened the lid, I had a view of the bottom of the canyon. Kind of gave me pause. At this point, Celeste and the other travelers had had enough of the switchback road, and I was outvoted—we were turning around. Celeste was cold, scared, and missing what she thought a Mexican vacation would be like. Never mind what I was thinking. In the morning we retraced our steps back to the Pacific, Martina and her foxy girlfriend, taking the train to Los Mochis and then flying to La Paz, a beach town on the Sea of Cortez. Unfortunately, we arrived just in time to catch the hurricane that had been sending the rain our way in the canyon. We spent the last few days getting sand-blasted in our loungers as the wind blew down upon us.

"This isn't working," I told Celeste. "I just can't date someone who is married." Actually, I was thinking, "I just can't date someone who does not love Mexico."

Virgin of Guadalupe, Oaxaca de Juárez, Oaxaca, 1992. Wood, 18 × 4.5 × 3.5 in. Private collection.

Learning Spanish

Oaxaca City, February 1992

MY ROOM IN the Hotel Marquiés del Valle overlooked the main square. Almost midnight, and children still lofted hot-dog-shaped balloons like javelins; street vendors sold popcorn, corn on the cob, shawls, and night-blooming flowers. A band with marimbas was still playing under the eaves. Because I was a railroader, I had earplugs, and I put them in. I could still hear the fireworks, but farther away.

Following a path of marigolds, I encounter a grave. A door opens, and my grandmother greets me. I am born again.

In the morning I found the house I would live in for six weeks while learning Spanish. I had tried to speak on the phone the day before with the family but failed to communicate who I was. I pushed the doorbell button on the glass and wrought iron double doors of 208 García Vigil. The smell of fresh bread invaded the air from Pan Bamby, the bakery across the street. The maid opened the door, and from behind her Guadalupe Pedroarona de Pisano (Lupita) took my hand and drew it to her cheek. Years rolled away, and the scent of my grandmother Ella came back to me, perhaps the only person I have ever completely loved. Lupita had her shape and the flowered housedress was surrounded by the kitchen odors with something always on the stove. She led me upstairs, through an open inner courtyard filled with huge pottery planters in iron stands, and up to a row of rooms above the courtyard, with insect-eaten wood doors, twenty-foot-high ceilings, and a small child's narrow bed, from which I could see clouds forming and dissolving in the Fiestaware blue sky.

Here were the roots of California architecture, the very flowers the same—bougainvillea, *guaje*, yucca, agave, plumeria, all living around me. My childhood house melded into the green stone of the buildings, the adobe walls, and the wild freedom of color. "To be Mexican is to be free," a boatman said to me once. I felt this from the first glance at my new home.

Lupita lived with Elda, her youngest daughter, who was my age. In the Mexican tradition, this daughter does not marry and instead cares for the mother. Elda, Marta María Pisano Pedroarona, was the director of a *jardín de niños*, a preschool, very near the house. She had a smoker's voice and laughed deep in her throat. It took her time to get it together in the morning, but that involved full makeup, a skirt, and heels. She drove a Volkswagen, loved parakeets, and hated cats, including Lupita's cat, Gaspar. She liked her liquor and singing boleros off key. I was very glad I had listened to Los Panchos driving to work and could sing with her. If I did not have sufficient water in my shower, she would climb up a wooden ladder on the roof to turn on the pump for the cistern, even while tipsy if necessary. All in skirt and heels.

"*Los hombres son tontos,*" she would tell me. Men are stupid.

"Yes," I thought, "but her world doesn't have alternatives."

We lived outside even in the house, since all doors were open to the courtyard. We were under roofs but breathing fresh air. The language school, run by a woman named Yolanda, was in another of these old mansions, and there I met my teacher, Marta, and I began to speak Spanish. Marta was a dentist who was making ends meet, but she was a born teacher. The method at the school was to jump into Spanish by answering basic questions, such as "How did you awaken this morning?" If you were invested in maintaining your dignity, you would have problems. Luckily I had embraced a return to childhood the moment Lupita answered the door, so I was happy learning to speak again. And Marta was yet another good mother. Since we students were by nature comical, she laughed along with us. I remember her teaching us the Guelaguetza dances of the seven regions of Oaxaca and how my dance of the bull made her laugh outright. It was role reversal—I was about twenty years older than my teacher. After four hours in school, I went back to the house for the big dinner of the day and spoke Spanish at the table. Lupita did the cooking, and every meal included black beans, which were always simmering in a ceramic pot on the stove. Other than that, mainly we had stews, with fava beans or the seven types of moles, or sauces, that Oaxaca is famous for. Every meal had five plates, which were changed for every course: a *sopa seca*, typically spagetti; salad; an entrée; beans; and dessert.

It was here that I learned how to eat a mango at the table. There is a little hole near the attachment of the stem that the middle prong of a fork will fit into. Now you have a mango on a fork. You then take a knife and make five lengthwise cuts in the skin and peel each one down. Now you have a peeled mango on a fork. You eat it. It's ripe and sticky. You then turn your fork over and tap the sticky seed with the dull side of your knife, and it falls on your plate with a plop.

During these two-hour meals, we conversed. I brought my dictionary along for help in the middle of conversations. It was

during the Monica Lewinsky crisis, and I had a lot of "'splaining"
to do.

"Why are they writing all that about the poor man's personal
life in the papers?" they wanted to know.

I, in turn, had a lot of questions about the soap opera they
watched every night, *Si Dios me quita la vida*. "What just happened?" I asked, after a dramatic pause during which the mother
of the house turned to the camera and grimaced.

"Well," Elda said, "her daughter just found out she was sleeping
with her boyfriend."

"*Sinvergüenza*," Lupita said. Without shame.

"Really?" I said.

Marta explained to me that everyone knew everything about
everyone in Oaxaca—for example, that the priest had a mis-
tress—but people overlooked it, particularly if it was someone in
a position of power. Like a president.

"Why do they care whom he is sleeping with?" she said.

"Because we hate sex and are obsessed with it," I said. I knew it
was unexplainable, like the reflexive construction in Spanish. "The
dishwasher broke itself," you might say. "The glass tipped itself
onto the floor." The language allows this. English wants causality
and blame.

Some days it seemed I could speak and be understood, and other
days I could hardly say a word. When I needed to speak English, I
would go to the zocalo, the town center, and find English speakers.
Sometimes I would just go into a church and cry. The sense of being
an outsider overwhelmed me. Mexican houses are all walled off on
the street side. You have to be invited inside to even see what they
are. At the market prices are doubled for foreigners. Street sellers
approach you constantly. And you are taller and bigger than everyone else. People call you "whitey," *güera*. Sometimes, it gets to be too

much. On the other hand, I felt very connected. I felt seen. I asked the woman who sold gum on the corner to embroider a flower over a hole in my T-shirt. She took it home with her, as it turned out, to Guelatao, a town up in the Sierra Juárez. I kept seeing her on the street, and she kept giving me that "in a moment" gesture of the thumb and first finger held parallel. After about three weeks, she pulled a plastic bag out from under her cart and returned my T-shirt with four embroidered yarn flowers around the neckline. It was much more elaborate than I had imagined. She started giving me gum after that. I would give her little gifts, a shell Virgin of Guadalupe, a silver thimble. I found out she had a daughter who was a teacher and a son lost in the United States. She hadn't heard from him in many years.

She asked me, "*¿Tienes tu casa?*" Do you own a home? She had hers up in the mountains.

The bed in my room was narrow and the mattress sagged, so I located a furniture repair store below the Benito Juárez market. I bought crossbeams and surreptitiously carried them two at a time up to my room, fortifying my mattress. I also went to a fabric store and bought a fake leopard fur bedspread. I couldn't do anything about the scorpions that rock-climbed up the walls, but Marta told me that in Oaxaca the cure for bites was to eat chocolate, so I had a few bars by my bed, just in case.

I inherited a few Mexican friends from a Santa Cruz friend named Barbara, who had told me to come to Oaxaca and who was the most charismatic person I had ever met. She connected with waiters, teachers, and people half her age, of all classes. Her Spanish was far from perfect, yet she was able to converse with people for hours. I, on the other hand, wanted to speak perfectly and had trouble talking over dinner. One of her American buddies, Lenore, was married to the Oaxacan who owned the mansion the school was in. They invited me to their house one afternoon, and I found myself discussing music with her husband. Again I was very glad I had listened to Los Panchos in my truck.

He was into superlatives. "The best voice in Mexican music is Pedro Vargas," he said. "And the best song is 'Peregrina' by Ricardo Palmerín. It tells the story of an American woman who fell in love with the governor of Yucatán. Surely you know it."

Barbara also knew Sadot, who was studying music at the Escuela de Bellas Artes, and his wife, Lizbeth, and their baby, Bruno. They invited me to his graduation, where he sang opera in the school building made of the green stone of colonial Oaxaca, called *cantera verde*. The old colonial name for Oaxaca was Verde Antequera. Sadot wanted to go to the United States to work. There just weren't any good jobs in Oaxaca for people who didn't have connections. Lizbeth, a fiery poet, wanted to stay. In the United States they would be "illegals." Here they had dignity. But here they would always work to just get by.

Barbara's other friends also visited me when they heard I was here. She had met Yvonne and Alan at the zocalo one day when there weren't any tables and she invited them to join hers. Yvonne told me they were suspicious at first because the gossip about Americans was that they stole children for organ transplants. Her parents said, "She was so much older than Yvonne; we didn't think she was an appropriate friend, but then we got to know her." Barbara had invited them to come visit her in Santa Cruz. Because her father, Alfredo, was a doctor in Tehuantepec, they could meet the stringent requirements for a visa, but they still had to go to Mexico City and wait in the around-the-block line at the American embassy. Then Barbara had to contact Leon Panetta, our local congressman, to intercede on the American end. He did, and Yvonne and her mother, Nina, went. Yvonne was studying in

Oaxaca to be a lawyer. One day, she invited me to go out to Reyes Etla to spend the afternoon with a friend of hers who lived on a ranch. It was a hot day, and we had taken shelter on the porch when her friend's father came in from the fields and quietly sat down in a leather chair. Within minutes, a servant brought him a tray with a pitcher of lemonade and a glass. While he sat there, silently drinking his lemonade, I was reminded of the B. Traven story of the Mexican hacienda owner and his American wife. She will not bring him his lemonade, and so, to shame her, he has to shoot his faithful horse in front of her, after rhetorically asking the horse to bring the lemonade.

I was in a meeting room, and the door curtains parted, and the most beautiful woman I had ever seen walked in.

"I am Danute, and I like to sleep with men I meet in the street."

She was just one day sober and started to hang around with me to stay that way. She was coming off a Mexican walkabout from Nayarit to Jalisco to Yucatán, sleeping with boys, chiefs of police, whoever approached her park bench on a drunken night in Mérida. I remembered driving at dawn with Veronica from Chichén to Cancún to return our car. We had passed a bus stop bench, and I thought I saw a woman in a red cocktail dress and high heels splayed over the bench, laughing.

Danute told me goddess stories. She was Kali, goddess of destruction, who sleeps with men to enlighten them. She was La Llorona, the crying ghost who walks at night.

"And then I met a man at a crossroads, and he said, 'Aren't you afraid to meet me here?' And I said, 'Aren't you afraid of meeting me?' And he ran away."

I didn't run away but listened in the car, her hand inches from my leg, as she talked and talked about sex. Oaxaca was transformed into a city heavy with desire, unrequited, adolescent. I was suddenly like the teenagers kissing in alcoves all over the city.

"It's OK," my teacher, Marta, told me. "If they are in public, they are not having sex."

I would go back to my little room at Lupita's house and have hot dreams along with Gaspar's feline howls until Elda threw a curse and a shoe and all was quiet.

I couldn't tell them all about my life. I didn't have the words, and I was unwilling to risk losing what I had found with the family. I settled into the Oaxacan way: don't ask, don't tell. This was a regression also, since I had already come out in the railroad world of men, where they literally could kill me. Here what I risked was loss of the mother figure, which seemed worse. I thought about Lupita's life, how she had never been alone, in the house, going to market, never, in her life alone. On the railroad I walked long trains at midnight in the desert all alone, waiting to meet another train, my lantern finding tarantulas and rattlesnakes, the moonlight my blanket, the oncoming train, a searchlight hidden within the twisting terrain, approaching us.

In El Llano Park, near my house in Oaxaca, in the morning I saw the sweepers making their brooms, braiding the branches. Later, coming back from my walk, I saw a delegation of villagers from the coast, with their drinking gourds and woven mats to sleep on. They wore backstrap-loom-woven white pants and shirts, bleeding with *caracol* dye. The house of the deputies, where Yvonne worked, fronted the park, and citizens from all parts came with grievances. In the moneyed world of the city, they were like ghosts or old spirits of the land. Still later, Elda and Lupita and I went to rescue their Chevy where it had died in Tule. We sat down near the oldest tree in the world and had hard bread marinated in fruit vinegar, along with drinks. A cousin had adjusted the carburetor, so all that remained was to drive it home. I did this with no license, following Elda as she ran the stoplights, and we arrived in time for dinner. Afterward, Lupita played the piano in the red-velvet-upholstered salon, which smelled of Gaspar.

I bought a little etched knife, a specialty of Ocotlán de Morelos, a town in one of the fingers of the central valleys. Its sheath was stitched and quickly came apart, so I took it to a leather repair store-front outside the Benito Juárez market. The little old man who ran the shop agreed that we could put rivets in the leather.

"Next week," he told me.

Next week I returned, but the shop was not there. I got lost looking for it. All the surrounding shops were where they were. I asked, but nobody knew anything about a leather shop, or they sent me to other locations blocks away, where there were lots of leather shops. About once a week, I tried to find the old man. I found other distractions—the woman who carried a basket of gardenias balanced on her head, the fragrance filling half the block; the man with a sisal bag of chicken feathers; the knife sharpener who used a bicycle wheel; and women selling *tlayudas*, large flour tortillas, nestled inside deep straw baskets in embroidered squares of cloth, like the one Juana the gum lady made for me. Other stalls contained coconut shell masks lacquered and made into the faces of jaguars, mermaids, devils, from Guerrero, the next state over. I bought a large jaguar mask with mirrors for eyes and holes at the sides for the strings with which to tie it on your head. Still no cobbler. Finally, with a week to go before I had to return to California, I was walking down the street, and the store miraculously appeared right where I thought it was to begin with.

"Yes, I have your sheath," he said happily.

What was lost was now found.

I had a crick in my neck from reading in the ancient bed. I took Barbara's advice and went to the public bathhouse down near the Central de Abastos market. A large steam room with wooden benches along the sides was filled with naked women speaking indigenous languages. From large, round shower heads on the ceiling hung chains that you could pull for ice-cold water. In the dressing room, two women offered massage, which consisted of one of them walking on my back followed by both of them wrapping me in a long towel and pulling on the ends, as if they were wringing laundry. This treatment made the crick in my neck worse.

I asked one of the wood-carvers who sold in the zocalo to make me an *alebrije*, a painted wood carving, of the Virgin of Guadalupe. It was also finished the week I had to go back to the States. I arrived in Oaxaca with a gym bag, and I left with a loaded basket that a donkey would have trouble carrying. I worried about the weight.

"Don't worry," Lupita told me, "the Virgin will take care of that."

We said good-bye, all of us crying at the airport. It was only later that I realized the Virgin was Lupita's name saint and I had made the image to take her with me.

I was back in the States, at an exhibit of the treasures of Teotihuacán at the Mexican Museum in San Francisco. I was sitting in the mini-auditorium listening to the Spanish-language summary, and the couple next to me was getting fidgety. "Why isn't this in English?" he was saying. Just a few minutes' wait, and it would be done. But the insult was that Spanish was given equal time. To have to listen to it at all.

I managed to take an accelerated Spanish class at Cabrillo College in Santa Cruz before the beet season started on the railroad.

Something had shifted, and I was seeing new images rising out of the world I lived in. Immersed in farmwork, I was on the crew that switched the loaded produce out of the packing warehouses in Salinas, the salad bowl of the world. I looked to guess where the pickers might be from. Oaxaca? I went to Mexican grocery stores and saw the black beans, the panela, or raw sugar, and the tamarind candy. These things allayed my homesickness for Mexico. Nobody asked me how I arose this morning. Nobody cooked me beans. I counted the days until I could return at Christmas, to yet another winter season on the railroad reserve board, paid not to do a job they wanted to get rid of.

No wonder that in Mexico I was drawn to those who do things like my anachronistic work: people carrying firewood, like what I use in my mountain cabin; bus drivers and their young money takers. My journal read:

> He named his bus *Obsession*, painted weathered cobalt with red memories. The driver looked fifteen, wearing jeans and a white t-shirt, the seat almost too big for him. The bus was even bluer inside, like a nightclub or a blue motel. Blue flashing lights circumnavigated the windshield, lighting up in clockwise pulses. Ink-blue fur cradled the rear-view, and dead center a double heart pulsed progressively red, green, yellow, and gold. All windows of the bus wore lapis blue fringe with white trim, and under the driver's hands, a candy-apple blue steering wheel and a crystal candy-apple blue shifter knob. Freedom of expression.

It was like the freedom I had on the railroad, the freedom a crew had to use all their skill and knock out the work, then play pinochle in a shanty hidden deep in the districts; to knock out the work some more, then snooze on overtime or park the engine on the mainline for a nightcap in a farmworkers' bar. Parallel lives, only now I have the linguistic key.

I went to a movie at the Nickelodeon Theatre in Santa Cruz and sat next to a Chamula man from Chiapas in his *jerkail*, a white, furry wool serape. Intersections. I passed a Huichol man in ceremonial dress on the street in Berkeley, carrying plastic grocery bags.

At Christmas, I went south to Chiapas to see Marcey and Janet. My new girlfriend came with me. I was trying again, but it was another disaster. Everyone in the world was in the Mexico City airport waiting for relatives. The porter had to make a path for us to pass through, and I saw her eyes glaze over. Later, she wouldn't come out of the room, except to buy Nicorette, the big draw in Mexico, apparently. Once in Chiapas, securing safe food became an issue, since her control was being shattered. A size zero, the nothing that she ate could not be reproduced here. I was again on the other end of the blaming glare. During the second non-meal, she ran out of the restaurant screaming.

"Does she know the way back to the hotel?" I thought. "Do I get to eat my enchilada?"

I later found her on the floor of our room, howling. Marcey's friends owned the hotel, and we were getting the friends and relatives rate. I was seriously rethinking this whole business of having girlfriends. But I couldn't mention this now. Marcey and Janet were very welcoming. If they thought I was bringing a crazy person to visit them, they didn't say anything. Janet was not doing too well, and they thought it was her electrolytes. I was wearing a long, padded silk coat, and I gave it to her when I left for Oaxaca. Janet's wardrobe was to die for, since other people had the same impulse to give her their clothes. One of her friends owned the Odyssey clothing store in Santa Fe, which was upscale hippie heaven.

The girlfriend flew home, and I was glad to leave the world of relationships behind when I arrived in Oaxaca and returned to my little room above Lupita's courtyard, although the supports I had snuck into the house for the bed mysteriously disappeared, probably downstairs to their beds. I replaced them. I was writing a novel now, with the central character modeled on my mother as a young woman, which turned out not to be such a good idea for fiction. As therapy, though, it was pretty interesting. The main things that had changed were that Danute was no longer in town, and Marta no longer worked for Yolanda at the school—she had her own school now. Of course, I followed her there. I wrote mornings, then, for an hour and a half after siesta, I met with her to ponder the imperfect subjunctive and read the local papers.

"It is corrupt," she told me, "*del pavimento a los cimientos*," from the floor to the ceiling.

We were talking about the practice of buying a professional degree.

"I did not buy mine," she said, "but others . . ."

This lined up with what I was noticing in the newspapers. There were lots of stories about scandal and corruption, but the last paragraph always stopped just short of offering a solution or even saying what happened to the perpetrators. There was never any follow-up. Marta's transition from teacher to school owner was not without problems. Her former employer, Yolanda, was taking her exit personally. After I told her I had followed Marta, when I passed her on the street she would not speak to me. She had a particularly crazy hateful stare, and she was everywhere. The English-language newspaper she put out, *Oaxaca Times*, now contained references to "second-rate" spurious language schools that foreigners were warned to beware of. Marta, like most people without a hateful bone in their bodies, was vulnerable to attack.

She hired a *curandera,* or healer, to perform a *limpia,* or cleansing, on her new school. We both thought this was a good idea, even though we didn't believe in limpias. Couldn't hurt, since Yolanda had clearly gone over to the dark side and was performing harmful rituals of her own. We now called her *la bruja,* or witch. The kinder term is *rara,* or odd. To be rare was, in Mexico, not as complimentary as it was in the United States. The collective society was still the value, and to be too individualistic was seen as threatening.

I met the legendary Mary Hester, the Texan who brought Alcoholics Anonymous to Oaxaca. She and her friend Mary Randall went with me to the Juárez market to eat *nieves,* the shaved ice and fresh fruit answer to Baskin-Robbins. The nieve boys gave her the same hard time they gave me, and I was reminded that seniority meant nothing when it comes to being a foreigner. We all just got off the boat. Mary told me stories of Mexican betrayal. She was married to a Mexican here, and after he died she tried to run their chicken business by herself. One day she took an agreed-upon load of chicks in a truck up the valley to Ocotlán, where the receiver offered her much less than they had agreed upon. She knew that he knew the chicks would all die on the way back and that she had no choice but to sell them. The temptation to cheat a woman just to do it was greater than to have her business. Later she worked for a magazine in Mexico City and built it up, only to be replaced by a Mexicana. I thought of the heartbreak of the photographer Tina Modotti, exiled from Mexico by the anti-Communist government, and I thought of my own love for Mexico and the heartbreak that probably awaited me.

My friend Mary Kate from Santa Cruz came down for a week to visit and couldn't make herself understood in her host family. They were worried that she was using their phone to call long

distance to the United States, so she came over to our house crying. Elda and Lupita called her *"la muchacha que lloraba,"* the girl
who cried. She brought over an American woman she met who
was in Mexico to go on a diet retreat. This struck me as really silly,
since so many people here had to struggle to get food. I saw how
gross our ideas put into motion could be: a $600 plane ticket,
hotels, some food guru organization, all mobilized so some vaca-
tioner could satisfy a loony idea of starving herself.

"Hope it goes well," I told the dieter.

Walking home after dark, I saw that there was a dance in the
Universidad Autónoma Benito Juárez facility in the plaza near my
house. I peered in the windows open to the street and saw
dressed-up young women and men sitting in chairs around the
empty dance floor. A boom box was playing "Amor a la mexicana"
by Thalia. A young woman wearing fishnet tights under a
G-string, high heels, and a black bra a la Selena was in the middle
of the floor performing a *cumbia*. It was the most erotic performance I have ever seen, her motions achieving isolation of each hip
in the circular motion I remembered from the time a friend I
thought I knew put her tongue in my mouth and hip rolled. Perhaps the sexiest and most unexpected kiss I have ever received.
Here it was now at the Facultád de Ciencias, the science school of
the university. As the saying goes, *Como Mexico, no hay dos*. There
are not two like Mexico.

Yvonne invited me to come with her to Tehuantepec and stay
with her family. She couldn't leave until early morning, so I went
down on my own, a four-hour bus ride south to the isthmus. My
Mexican family warned me about going. Oaxacans were sure that
people living elsewhere in Mexico were backward.

"The people there are dirty and lazy," they said. "And there are
thieves on the road."

I knew this was true, because I had started reading the papers. Bandits, often in collusion with bus drivers, put tires across the highways in remote locations and robbed night buses.

I asked Yvonne if she was afraid of bandits.

"Oh yes," she said. "But I'm Catholic and I pray to the Virgin."

So when I got on the bus, I prayed to the Virgin and said, "Look, I'm not Catholic, but everyone else on this bus is, so don't let us get robbed."

The road wound and wound in the dark, always downward. We descended 5,000 feet before the land evened out a little, and we crossed a big river that didn't cascade but was slow moving. The moon was full, and I had a window seat, so I could see a train paralleling our road. It seemed to go under us and reemerge alongside, like an articulated dragon; for me it was a welcome friend. Later, in an art gallery in Oaxaca, I saw a painting of this same train in the form of a sea serpent diving and surfacing into a salty lagoon. The artist was from Tehuantepec.

The railroad ran directly in front of Yvonne's family home—so close that if there were to be a derailment, the train would land in their living room. Her father, Alfredo, walked me there from the humid bus station, where I got off at 2:00 a.m. and didn't know another soul. They put me in the only room that had a bed. Everyone else slept in hammocks in the other rooms, nobody but me noticing the Japanese clock that rang every hour with a different song as I lay in my pool of sweat. Yvonne arrived sometime during the night, and in the morning we put plastic chairs in the back of their pickup truck and rode past coconut palms and mango groves to a natural spring, where we swam while majestic women in long skirts served sweet bread and coconuts with straws.

"*Oro de Tehuantepec*," Yvonne's father said, noticing me

drinking from a coconut—gold of Tehuantepec. "Now you will always return."

Looking at my passport, I can see he was right. I have returned to Mexico every year at least once, sometimes more.

The next day we were invited to a party, isthmus style. We walked over a concrete bridge spanning the river, where women were washing clothes and hanging them on bushes. The party was all women, except for Alfredo and the male musicians. The women were wearing their traditional isthmus velvet outfits minus the head skirt, which was only for extra-special occasions. Everyone drank a lot, and I saw several women goose the mariachi players. The hostess saw me notice this and came over to our table.

"I am sorry," she said, "but *así son mi gente*," this is how our people are.

I had heard that the isthmus was a matriarchy where women did all the business, being tall and stately and wearing gold filigree jewelry as they rode on the front platform of bicycle carts pedaled by skinny men in white shirts and pants. It was indeed so. When we went to the market where Nina, Yvonne's mother, had a stall, her friends came up to me and demanded to know where I was from and why didn't I invite Yvonne to come visit me in California.

"We did go," Nina said, and that shut them up.

"Thank you, Barbara," I thought, "for bringing them to the States."

Nina made more money in her market stall than Alfredo made as a doctor. "*Una chamba pequeña, una vida buena,*" a little gig, a good life, she told me.

Before we caught the bus back to Oaxaca, the family pulled out a gift they wanted me to take back to the States, an alabaster desk ornament of two owls separated by pen holders. It must have weighed fifty pounds. It reminded me of Mussolini's "typewriter" building in Rome. Inscribed in its stone base was the name Leon Panetta.

This was the return gift for the visit arranged by Barbara. Looking around their house, there wasn't much evidence of affluence. Owls are the traditional symbol for lawyers, so it was possible that Panetta was getting a gift originally meant for Yvonne. My reception was probably part of it all. Unfortunately, I was planning on traveling to Chiapas and Guatemala, and I could not carry this cargo with me, so I reluctantly refused. They didn't seem fazed. They were absolutely certain that Leon Panetta would get his owls, and if it wasn't now then it would be sometime in the future. I thought this belief was really Mexican, the quality that made daily life in Mexico so positive.

While Barbara and I were perfectly free to come visit Mexico from California, the opposite was not true. Congressional intervention for a two-week visit? Most of my Mexican friends, who were not doctors or professionals, could never get a visa. They had to have $2,000 in a bank account in their name. And even if they did have that, it would mean an all-day wait in a line at the embassy in Mexico City. More expenses for travel to the capital, a hotel, eating out. No wonder that, to Mexicans, North Americans on their beach vacations seemed oblivious. The border gate swung only one way.

I saw what the riders on our desert trains were leaving behind: beauty, family, culture, but no work. No irrigation for agriculture. No potable water. No opportunity to better yourself through education. North American thirst for drugs ruining any chance of a good Mexican government.

Barbara later told me about how the owl got to the United States.

"Ultimately my doctor released me to travel in Mexico again, and I went to Tehuantepec one more time, and here is the owl with Leon Panetta's name on it, and they wanted me to bring it back, and I said, 'It's too heavy, I can't take it,' and they said, 'Leon Panetta has to have it, and we went to a great deal of expense to have this made for him, and you have to help us get it to the US.' So I carried this fifty-pound owl back to Oaxaca; carried it on the plane, because I was afraid to ship it; had to change planes in Mexico City; carried it around all day; and finally put it on the second plane."

Of course, when she finally got it to the United States, Leon Panetta was in Washington, DC, and he couldn't accept gifts. But it will get to him eventually, if God wills it.

Before I had to return to my job for the summer rush, I planned to visit Chiapas and then go traveling to Guatemala, since I could now speak Spanish. This time on the ride to the airport for my flight to Chiapas, Elda had a little crash with another car trying to get into her lane. There was a dent on Lupita's side, but neither of them appeared to be very upset. We all cried again at the airport.

Xela, Guatemala, April 1993

When I set out to travel to Guatemala, Janet and Marcey asked me to carry some *duraznos*, or peaches, from Chiapa de Corzo along as a present for their friend Joan Ablon, an anthropologist who studied physical disabilities, who was working in Antigua. They came in a little wooden box, nailed shut. A sweet prune. I was going to travel as long as I could before the railroad called me back to work. A woman named Susan told me about a town called Todos Santos Cuchumatán, where she worked in a language school. She said it was really beautiful but she had to leave because of politics. By this she meant threats. The civil war was very brutal in the highlands, with the Guatemalan army following a policy very much like ours in Vietnam. This was not a coincidence, since their officers were trained in Georgia at the School of the Americas, which taught counterinsurgency tactics to foreign army specialists. She showed me some of the weaving from there, and I was hooked. What babies we are, North Americans. A cave climber with shot knees, Mike Boone, told me about a hotel in Huehuetenango, a jumping-off place for Todos Santos: Hotel Central. I wrote it in my little book. Janet and Marcey drove me to the border—stopping, of course, in Teopisca for *costillas*, or pork ribs. Their map of Mexico was a meat map—ribs here, T-bone steak there. Things they never ate at home. As we drove down the valley, banana trees appeared, and the rocky outcrops stood like teeth among them. I felt the road opening indefinitely before me, the Pan-American, all the way to the end of the continent.

I walked across the border and got my passport stamped in the wooden immigration shack. All around money changers mobbed me. It turned out that the only places that would change pesos to quetzals were barbershops, the governments of both countries making it hard for people to cross easily. I caught a bus for Huehue, an old Blue Bird school bus, repurposed. The bus kept picking up passengers until the aisle was standing room only. At intervals everyone in the aisle would duck down so that it looked like the bus was not overcrowded. Going up mountains, we stopped at waterfalls to cool the radiator. All cargo was tied on top, but I had a slim duffle that I managed to keep inside with me. At stops, cargo was thrown off, and if you saw your bag being unloaded, you really could not get out to grab it.

Hotel Central at dusk was nothing to write home about. It was so central that dust from the highway blew through it all night, the thin blanket they gave me doing little to keep off the chill. Ditto for the door latch, supposedly for keeping out thieves. A hook and eye. I already longed for Marcey and Janet's electric blanket, which they loaned out to friends. I had already stopped off at the second-class bus station to get my ticket for tomorrow, a window seat. Those were my rules. Start out early and get a window seat.

Plainly, the man and his wife sitting on the bus when I got on the next morning were sitting in my window seat. They ignored my awkward hovering and hunched closer to the wall. I took the remaining seat, on the aisle, perhaps the biggest mistake of my life. All the seats were taken, and then the aisle filled up. Indigenous Maya people in traditional dress kept getting on. Children were stowed under the seats. On the aisle, I was getting smashed, but I wasn't giving up the perfectly good space in front of my knees that several children could have occupied. At this point, an ice cream seller pushed onto the bus and started passing *paletas*, popsicles, over our heads. Other food sellers got on. The man in my window seat pretended to be sleeping. At last, we started up the mountain. For three hours nobody on the bus would open a window, and it started to rain hard. Some of the seats were really just boards, and they started to slide backward. Finally, at the summit, some people got off, relieving the pressure a little. Great, since I was tired of being regarded as a space criminal. At last we descended into the little valley that holds Todos Santos, passing a quixotic guard post with homespun-dressed citizens holding ancient one-shot rifles. All the roofs had blue plastic ducks on them. I found a hotel on the dirt main street with equally thin blankets and walls that did not go all the way to the ceiling. People had loud domestic conversations all night, as if they had privacy. I couldn't get another blanket. "Toughen up," the proprietor's look said.

When I started to get a picture of what this town had been through, I could ease off my discomforts a bit. A guide from Susan's language school showed me around and told me what had happened when the army attacked the town. We were in the church at the time, the ceiling covered with frescoes of fat angels in brightly colored cowboy boots. Those angels had seen the townspeople locked in there, wondering if they were going to be set on fire, while others were dragged off and tortured. In Nobel Peace Prize winner Rigoberta Menchú's book *I, Rigoberta Menchú*, the Guatemalan writer described the trucks the indigenous Maya rode in to go pick coffee on plantations. Her description made me realize that the bus I'd been on, however crowded, was a luxury ride. Now all the men were required to participate in the home guard, actions that could get them in trouble with the rebels, who were still in the area. The people were in a dangerous middle zone.

The weaving was truly magnificent. Everyone wore it, red and purple and blue thickly woven patterns, with red striped pants for the men and red striped shirts with brocaded collars and cuffs. I went for a sauna at a weaver's house, and the door of the outdoor oven-like steam room was a beautiful weaving. Art was integrated into daily life and used. But it was that very quality that marked the indigenous people as targets. Some had become Protestants as cover from the army and begun to wear Ladino dress, which is what the Maya called Western clothing. Ladinos spoke Spanish and did not identify as Indian.

The last night before I left, I ate at Tres Olguitas, named for three sisters named Olga. Normally their food was great, but in this instance, it was not. Still sick as a dog the next morning, I got on the bus one more time, and when we reached Huehue I crawled into a more institutional hotel, where I continued to be sick as a dog all night again. Of course, the bathroom was down the hall. The next day, slightly better, I took another bus for Quetzaltenango, or Xela, as it was locally called. We went through the usual packed-in and then ducking-down scenario. A man in the aisle started to hit a woman seated in front of me. He looked my size, and I stood up. Then other people on the bus, including women, chastised him for being brutal "in front of a stranger," meaning me. Of course I was an idiot to think I could have stopped him, but I was, after all, under the influence of the railroad, where you don't just open a door—you yank it open and kick it shut.

Guatemala had a different vibe from Mexico, probably because of the civil war. There was not the sound of a constant fiesta, and people seemed traumatized. I was still receiving a lot of help from strangers, however. Asking directions of an elderly woman, I was abashed when she went blocks out of her way to show me. Leaving my passport and money in a store, I heard my name called on the street; the shopkeeper ran after me to return it. Some walls held rebel graffiti, which I read in the local paper posed problems for the owners. If they rubbed it out, they were targeted. If they didn't, the army would visit them. Other dangers, I read, had to do with child adoption. North Americans were adopting indigenous babies, but in some cases the children had been kidnapped or had parents murdered by the army. On the street, this translated into the old rumor of children being stolen for organ transplants. I thought these rumors were probably planted by the army, since North American women often showed up in helper organizations as witnesses to the army's violence. What better way to get rid of the witnesses? I was of that demographic—so I was particularly careful not to touch children or really even look at them, which was hard, since they all wanted to touch my hair or just stare at my blue eyes. George Lovell, a political geographer, wrote a book titled *A Beauty That Hurts: Life and Death in Guatemala*. I was finding that to be true.

There couldn't be a greater beauty than the green volcanoes of the highlands and their cornfields being worked by indigenous men in traditional clothing in the misty morning. The men wore straw cowboy hats and simply knotted a square of plastic over their shoulders against the afternoon rain. The women's dress was an explosion of color, in contrast to the sere palette of Chiapas: rainbow colors in skirts and huipils, with carrying cloths adding different directional patterns to the total ensemble. At Lake Atitlán, I was boarding the launch to cross when the most exquisitely dressed woman I had ever seen got on. Barefoot, with a metallic ikat-thread wrap skirt, a handwoven huipil in reds, oranges, and purples, an ikat rebozo, and a carriage that suggested she could balance loads on her head with ease. She had a slanted Maya head shape that looked like the royals on the stelae and almond-shaped eyes. She would have not been underdressed for an opera in San Francisco. I could only gaze.

"They think we are walking huipils," a Maya activist has said.

In Xela I discovered that Joan's duraznos had not survived the trip. The sturdy wooden box was crushed in the bottom of my duffle, and peach paste was all over my clothes. Just as well, since I could not find Joan at the address in Antigua, and it was there that I got my call back from the railroad. I had two weeks to get home. Janet had referred to Guatemala as "the land of the lotus eaters," and Marcey had told me she would never set foot in it because of the repressive government. I found myself asking what I would have to ignore to live here while all this was going on. I was on the yellow brick road of tourism, giving money to weavers and local hotels and restaurants. My presence added to the immediate safety of those around me, yet after I left, the opposite might be true. It was complicated.

Lino Mora, Moor Mask, Naolinco, Veracruz, 1995. Wood, 11 × 9.5 × 8 in.
Private collection.

A Time of Desperation

Chiapas, January 1994

Cerulean,
Bluer and duller and greener and lighter and stronger,
The color of the sky
On January first, 1994, in Chiapas.

DRIVING TO THE San Jose, California, airport, a car cut me off on the mountain highway.

"You can't kill me, you bastard, I have cancer!"

I was meeting Leslie Marmon Silko in Mexico City, where we would be escorted to Chiapas for the second National Democratic Convention of the Zapatistas. Taped up from surgery and waiting on the doctors to form their plan, I was entering a year of magical thinking. The filling of the town of San Cristóbal de las Casas with 20,000 indigenous people in ski masks marching peacefully in the streets set the tone. I let go of who I thought I was and surrendered to the journey to the underworld. Change came. Later, when I began treatment back at home, I laid out Mexican objects like a sand painting that I was in the center of—four directions, protector animals, colors, old stories.

"In the middle of the journey of this life, I found myself in a dark wood," I told my chemo doctor as he slipped the needle into my hand.

He went along, and wore a bear suit for a photo op at journey's end. It was not the worst year of my life. I wrote a book. I lay on a mattress outside under the trees, as California allowed this. I saw them lose their leaves and find them again.

Oaxaca City, June 1995

When I was over the chemo, I had a corn-planting ceremony in Donna's garden in Santa Cruz to mark the end of treatment, and that night I had a dream that I was in an airport and they had lost my suitcases. I was back in the normal world. I went to Mexico with Barbara. Even though Mexico was full of potential infections, the slow pace was what I needed, and I needed to be around my two families: Lupita and Elda, Marcey and Janet. Barbara and I had the upstairs rooms, and the salon filled up as all her friends came over to visit us, Nina and Alfredo up from Tehauntepec, and Lizbeth, Sadot, and little Bruno. Barbara had appointments with all the waiters at the Marqués del Valle restaurant, and she wanted to go dancing at Candela at night. I was jealous of how she could talk with everyone, and I made some snotty remark about her Spanish. It is one of my regrets. Nobody cares how perfect your Spanish is. Barbara was worried about Lizbeth and her future since she was not trying to get a professional job. She paid Marta, our Spanish teacher who was also a dentist, to repair Lizbeth's teeth and to give her English lessons, but Lizbeth was too passionate to get in line for a future. She wanted it now. I got a cold right away, and it put me in dreamland. Walking down the street, I was hypersensitive to color, the cobalt blue paint on the white walls, the fuchsia flowers spilling over the red tile, the hot sun sterilizing everything.

Suddenly, I noticed a truck pull up to the building across the street, which was a nursing home. I had walked past it many times, seeing rags drying in the open windows and medical equipment in the rooms. Two men got out of the truck and climbed the stairs. Still watching, I saw them come down with a dead naked man between them, one of them holding his legs, the other, his arms. They walked to the back of the truck and swung the body up into the truck bed, his balls swinging in the wind. Then they got in the truck and drove away.

Mexico has a surreal way of bringing life and death together as halves of a single shell.

I crossed the street to walk in the shadow of the adobe walls. I was here now. I knew I was going to stay alive and bloom again.

Chiapas, July 1995

I went on to Chiapas again and stayed with my friends Janet and Marcey for another month, getting sick from mold but being surrounded by love. I was in their casita, their guesthouse, whose renter, Jim Breedlove, a retired Stanford University book buyer, was on a vacation. Janet later said, "We thought you wanted to be left alone, but then we realized you needed company." Janet was working on her Ocosingo swallows drawings, relating to the breakout and aftermath of the Zapatista revolution. One day she laid her series out for me along the walls of her studio, swallows flying in Yeatsian gyres, then giving way to black tornadoes of chaos in geometric shorthand. She moved slowly with shaking hands.

"You are probably thinking," she said, "how can she even hold a pencil?" Which was exactly what I was thinking.

We were always in and out of the past. Parking at Chamula, Marcey said, "One year they decided to charge to park, and I thought it was wrong, so I wouldn't pay—and they pulled Janet out of the car and took her to jail." She giggled. An irrepressible smile. "So I paid the five pesos."

Another day Janet and I went to a show of new artists at Santo Domingo Church. It is a hike down and up the hill they live on, but Janet made it with her cane in spite of the wet, slick stones and high curbs. They were both showing me how to be alive. Another day we all visited Na Bolom. Their friend Trudi had died, and her room was turned into a museum of her possessions. Janet and I peered in the gated door at her open closet, packed with outfits.

"That's known as taking it with you," Janet said. Marcey, impatient, was leaning on the horn in the street. Janet was ignoring her.

We went down to the town of Venustiano Carranza to visit a friend of theirs and ate lunch under a flamboyant tree at a roadside restaurant. We saw the black Jesus of Esquipulas in the church, and Janet and Marcey were both wearing pink, and at one point Marcey took her hand. I have that in a photograph, and it looks as though they were about to go to a ball.

There was a "ladies' hiking society" in San Cristóbal, consisting of the German expats, primarily. Hiking for pleasure was not a Mexican or indigenous concept. You walked to get somewhere, and sometimes it involved climbing mountains. Since this was after the Zapatista uprising, hiking was now even more suspect. We were headed down to the natural water park at el Egipto, near Chiflón, for a picnic—Marcey and Janet, me, a local artist and author named Kiki Suárez, and her husky dog. We passed a military checkpoint, and I realized I didn't have my passport. The soldier looked in the car, saw old ladies and the dog, and he waved us through. The water came into the swimming hole from two natural springs. Ceiba trees dipped their red roots into the underworld. As we ate our lunch, an old man was trimming the grass with a shears, blade by blade.

Before I left Chiapas in August, I invited Marcey and Janet to the grill down the street for ribs. At home they usually ate vegetables and chicken, but eating out, step back.

"*Arrachera con frijoles charros,*" Janet ordered. "*Y papas rellenas al horno.*" Steak with rancher's beans and stuffed baked potatoes.

"*Lo mismo,*" Marcey said. The same.

I really enjoyed paying the bill.

Finally, I went home to California, ready to face going back to work on the railroad.

The railroad was like the military in many ways. One of them was that you couldn't admit weakness or they would try to kick you out. I wanted to get back in, but I really needed light duty for a year. That would consist, on the railroad, of being put in a room with the book of rules and being told to read it. An exercise in shame. And so I went to a railroad doctor who asked me, "Are you OK?" "Yes," I said, and he approved me to return to work. Neither he nor I had any idea if I was ready or not. Actually, I was not. The railroad at the time was sending workers with my miserable seniority away from home twenty days a month to work eight hours on, eight hours off, around the clock. In February, seven months before, I had been so anemic I was unable to make my bed and needed daily shots to rescue my white blood count. I had no business now being called to work all night in strange locations. Luckily, I got a work train assignment the first month. That meant I could sleep at night. After that, in October, I caught an assignment out of Oakland that was mostly all-nighters. My old friend and braking partner John Payne was up there also and looked after me on the job. I needed it. My brain was literally fried. I made all kinds of simple mistakes, any one of which could have been lethal. We weren't playing with TinkerToys. I scheduled my vacation for November to give me more time to get better. Of course, I went back to Mexico.

Guadalajara, November 1995

This time old friends lined up to meet me there and spend a week. I see now they were thinking I might relapse and they would never see me again. I went to Guadalajara first to see Danute, the free Canadian I had met in Oaxaca in 1992. She was living in Ajijic and painting. Danute was perhaps the sexiest woman alive, and just being around her was guaranteed to wake you up to sexuality again. It did. I think sex and fear cannot coexist—so Mexico had its desired effect, immediately calling me back to life again. Life that was possible to live in, unlike my current railroad noir existence. Danute and I went shoe shopping at night in Guadalajara—a local pastime.

"Everyone spends all night looking at shoes," I said. "Why so many shoe stores?" The answer was León, the shoe capital of Mexico, just a few hours away. I bought some red patent-leather Mary Janes with Cuban high heels.

"Only someone like you could wear them," she said, crossing her legs and watching me try them on and walk up and down before her. I set them up as an altar on top of the TV, with a sequined Virgin of Guadalupe iron-on patch propped up inside one, reminding me of José Clemente Orozco's ships in the mural down the street.

The bus that took me to the suburb of San Pedro Tlaquepaque was named *Mil Amores*, A Thousand Loves. It was noon on the day my friend Margo was to arrive, and I was on a park bench in a little square in the perfect climate of Guadalajara in the early dry season of November. I was thinking about Danute. Then I noticed a large woman in a flowered dress, long black hair in a braid, lying down in the fountain, her legs hooked above the water jets, laughing. A man and two children were seated on the granite lip, pointedly looking the other way. An aspect of Danute, no doubt, like the voyaging bus and the red shoes.

By 3:00 p.m., Margo still had not arrived. A 7:00 I called Mexicana Airlines once, her house twice, our friend Donna twice. At 9:00 I called immigration at the airport, Mexicana in Mexico City. At 9:30 Donna called to say nobody had answered at Margo's house. Sleeping was difficult. I had a dream that I was in a railroad hotel and everybody was robbed. In the morning I called the US consul general, and he told me, "Madam, some people come to Mexico to get lost."

"Well, some people come to Guadalajara to get murdered," I said, thinking of Cardinal Juan Jesús Posadas, archbishop of Guadalajara, who was the victim of a cartel shootout at the airport two years before. I went to the airport and met the flight she should have been on the day before, and there she was.

"I was the last person in line at the airport, and I got bumped," she said. "Somebody's relative wanted to come. I mean he was on standby and getting dressed as he ran across the tarmac. Buttoning his shirt. Anyway, they said they would telex Mexicana so that you would know."

Of course, they hadn't. And later Margo called my hotel, but they didn't tell me. Or couldn't. As I had learned, English messages often did not get delivered.

The next day we took the bus to Morelia, where we installed ourselves in the Hotel Virrey de Mendoza, an old, balconied building with someone playing a grand piano in the lobby below. We slept like Christians in our stone room. The following morning at 6:00 Margo heard a tuba in the street below. A woman was walking down the middle of the street, carrying a box. Behind her were three tuba players. The mystery was cleared up when we arrived at our next destination, Lake Pátzcuaro, to see bandstands being erected in front of the hotel where we were to stay.

"It's Saint Cecilia's Day," the desk clerk told us. "Patron saint of music. Later there will be a battle of the bands."

Deep into a nap I thought I heard Margo say something about a maid and mopping. The band woke me in the manner of a Japanese alarm clock, and I jumped out of bed to do a few salsa steps. The thick carpet was sopping wet, and I was wearing socks.

Margo looked amused. "I said the maid was mopping the carpet."

Music followed us all weekend, whether we liked it or not. Eating breakfast, Margo tipped a Purépecha violin player, expecting him to move on. Instead he entered into another chorus of "The Dance of the Viejitos," sawing and hopping. He was ubiquitous. Every meal he saw us and rushed over. Even in the boat to Janitzio Island. "Revenge," I thought, "for my busking days."

Lake Pátzcuaro was, like Oaxaca, another crafts center of Mexico. Each little town specialized in a unique craft, such as ceramic devils in Ochumichu, straw sculptures in Ihuátzio, guitars in Paracho, and copper in Santa Clara del Cobre. Santa Clara had more than 200 copper workshops, where they crafted everything from handmade-bead necklaces to large cooking pots to silver-inlaid plates to hammered pots in pre-Hispanic pottery designs. What took my fancy this trip was a two-headed coyote pot so heavy and so expensive that I had to hit the ATM, conveniently located on the corner, to get more cash. "Unbreakable," was my thought. Somehow I imagined it as looking like the wolf mother of Romulus and Remus, the founders of Rome.

I almost missed my chance to buy the coyote pot, because we almost didn't make it to Santa Clara. Margo and I didn't recognize that Villa Escalante was the town's official name, and we didn't get off the bus in time. When we realized our mistake, we had to jump off on the mountain road to try to catch one going the other way. It was high and windswept rocky terrain, the clouds threatening rain, and we stood beside the road for a long time, waiting. A truck arrived and pulled in next to us, carrying young men in the back. We felt their eyeballs taking us in. A sense of secrecy and menace was in the air. We felt radically out of place, as if our presence was being debated. Finally they left, and a dusty bus going our way appeared down the road. Michoacán had this edginess outside the tourist route.

The best art in Pátzcuaro was the straw furniture by Mario López. It was in FONART stores all over Mexico, particularly his reproductions of Maya jaguar thrones. Mario created life-sized mandrills, birds, crocodile storage chests, saguaro cacti with copper-eyed birds nesting in their cavities. Margo and I bought small jaguar footstools modeled on the one from Chichén Itzá. Erongarícuaro, across the lake, was the home of an unusual furniture factory where locals painted European masters onto hand-carved wooden furniture, which was then lacquered. Two Americans, the Rosenthals, had started the factory, which was now an artist's cooperative. It was lucky that the airlines had not yet imposed weight or size limits on baggage. If you could get it on the plane, it flew.

The presence of all these crafts, representing the slowness of time that makes art possible, slowed us down. We could be in the moment with them. To look at them was a reward. The promise was that an artistic life was possible.

After Margo went back home, I attended the Ballet Folklórico de México in the Degollado Theater, just a few blocks from the Hotel Francés in Guadalajara. Guadalajara had a series of pedestrian blocks culminating in an eighteenth-century orphanage, now a museum, adjacent to the market. It was a matinee, and I felt surrounded by North Americans, although that was not true, since by the second act it was almost a full house, uncles bringing nephews, a family event, clearly. But the first two rows were blocked off initially, and just when I was feeling the familiar sense of the tourist, twenty dwarves came in and sat in those rows. Afterward I wandered, one of those days of feeling doubly erased, foreign, dressed wrong, too old, outside, and unplaceable. And yet, looking around me, I could see there was everyone, the crippled, the poor, the drunk, the rich, the well-to-do families, performers filling every public space and vendors following them, and so there was room, I started to feel, for me. At that point a well-dressed middle-aged man walked past me carrying a crepe paper swan. I joined the river of souls, following at a discreet distance until, almost at my hotel door, a man in his sixties, passing opposite me, caught my eye and said, "*Wunderbar.*"

Mexico City and Veracruz, November 1995

After Margo left, my friend Martie joined me in Mexico City. Martie had worked for the Southern Pacific until she fell and embedded a piece of ballast in her arm. She decided the railroad was not worth the risk and went back home to Portland. We were going to Veracruz on the bus, since the train had stopped passenger service. Before we left, we went to a concert at the Hotel Camino Real in Mexico City. Armando Manzanero and Tania Liberdad were singing songs from their famous duet album, *La Libertad de Manzanero*. The concert started around 11:00 p.m. The stage was set like an opera, and within minutes I believed both performers were singing about their romantic life together. We felt seriously underdressed. The anemone audience swayed with the tidal movements of the songs. This was a gift for Martie, since she was a folk singer with the ability to key into emotion in her listeners. The performance ended at 2:00 a.m., but no one in the crowd was tired. As we left the hotel, men and women were singing snatches from their favorite songs amid pirouettes.

Our destination in Veracruz was a result of my own obsession with the Mexican movie *Danzón*, which I had seen for the first time in Oaxaca. The film centered around a telephone operator in the Districto Federal, Julia, whose passion was danzón. Our hotel overlooked the plaza, where at 6:00 p.m. dancers assembled. Claiming a chair in the front row was the prerogative of the regulars, who arrived an hour in advance to be seated where they might be asked to dance. It was a SilverSneakers crowd that also included young people; the middle group was not represented. Dark-skinned men in panama hats, guayabera shirts, and white pants and shoes. Women in Yucatec huipils or spaghetti-strapped white dresses with the Mexican equivalent of tango shoes. They carried wooden fans. The band slowly set up under the ceiba-shaded bandstand. Harp, *guitarrón*, marimba, drums, guiro, baritone clarinet, flute. The couples assembled facing the bandstand, standing through the opening bars until, all together, they turned to face each other and began. The dance looked like a basic square, but there was an extra hesitation that led into the next figure and, at the end of a sequence, a rush to close. A young couple did what looked like tango flourishes with dips. I admired them to the woman standing next to me, who introduced herself as Carmen.

"Oh yes," she said. "They are innovative, but afterward the criticism," and she rolled her eyes. "How do you like my land, *mi tierra?*"

"Enchanted," I said.

"Do you know the movie?"

"That's why we're here."

"Well, the lead dancer in the movie, Daniel, is from here. He is not an actor, he's a dancer. The boardinghouse María Rojo stays in is right down that street."

Carmen told me she had worked in the United States but missed home too much. Her T-shirt said, "Three generations of danzón Veracruz."

The music had picked up. One of the instruments, the baritone clarinet, was oddly out of tune, which should have detracted but somehow didn't, like the quirkiness of a friend. The last part of the dance, Carmen told me, was the *montuno*, which was where the cha-cha-cha and mambo came from. To the fast beat, the dancers maintained a formal motionless position above the waist, but the Latin motion was happening from the waist down. Even the older couples could really rock.

Martie was a sharp dresser, but not in the feminine style. Long folk-singer hair, slim, and sporting a trademark O'Farrell 100 percent beaver hat, with beaded hatband. Veracruz was having a craft expo, FONART style, with objects from every region. We walked the aisles, admiring abalone-inlaid wooden boxes from Ixmiquilpan, guayaberas from Yucatán, and, in particular, a mask display by Lino Mora from Naolinco, just up the road.

His Moor mask for "The Dance of the Moors and the Christians" was a varnished maroon color, with white fangs and beard. The snake encircling its head was downright gleeful. Both snake and Moor looked like they had scored some great drug. Like William Blake's "Tyger! Tyger! burning bright." Since reading William Carlos Williams's opening sentence to "The Destruction of Tenochtitlán" I have thought of the Conquest as a wave sweeping down the Iberian Peninsula and continuing until it flooded the Americas: "Upon the orchidian beauty of the new world the old rushed inevitably to revenge itself after the Italian's return."

The Moor's face was both dark and Semitic—the Catholic Satan of the Reconquista, but danced in the New World. The beard, however, was an attribute of the conqueror. The sacred snake of the Americas was transformed into the companion of the Spanish devil, the native earth lord taking on his attributes while at the same time accruing new power. I stood staring at the mask as the artist watched me.

"It is not for sale," he said. "I need it for a competition."

"It will win," I told him. His glance took us in. Particularly Martie's hat, as it turned out.

That night in our hotel, the marimba from the street and the noise from the cafés competed with the face of the Moor to keep me in and out of sleep.

"I dreamed about it," I told Lino the next day when we returned.

"Well then, I have to sell it to you," he said immediately. "But just give me the hat of your amigo in trade," intentionally using the masculine ending.

"I would if it were mine," I said, "but it belongs to my amiga." Martie just pointedly looked elsewhere. In her calculation the mask was not the winner.

"Ah," he said, "well then, I will take money. Come and see me in Naolinco at my studio sometime," giving me his card.

Taking this ambiguous devil back home with me, after my own journey to the underworld, seemed to be a good idea. I had earned the totem, and perhaps I could draw power from the ways I was the devil to my opponents. I was thinking railroad.

Oddly enough, after I had surrendered to my inability to stay working on the railroad and found a temporary haven in the San Jose freight yard, Mora's mask reappeared to me. California has a long history of Mexican labor, starting, of course, when it was part of Mexico. Since those days, people have moved back and forth across the line in the sand, the railroad being the road to ride. By the 1990s the Santa Clara and Salinas valleys had mostly converted from agribusiness to high tech, but remnants remained, and pickers still came with the seasons. They also worked other jobs, but Silicon Valley salaries made rentals out of reach, so they slept on mattresses beside the rails, in the Hotel Mira Estrellas, the Hotel Look at the Stars. Since the railroad runs behind facades, I saw these workers and others who lived in tucked-away trailer parks, such as the one on Coyote Creek.

The industry track at Graniterock ran along the creek, which kept its natural shape. I always felt the presence of the invisible people in the trailer park, off the grid of Silicon Valley, hidden inside its industrial maze. I would sometimes look into the woods by the creek bank, amazed that something natural could continue its life here. Gang graffiti covered the warehouse walls facing the tracks, and tag crews often marked the cars in the small switching yard. One artist, however, had taken his time. The entire sloping rear porch of a cement hopper was covered with a detailed black-and-white portrait of Lino Mora's Moorish devil.

I was in a web of connections that I could see as a safety net, the way repetitive language works in poetry to convey an ambiguous sense of meaning. My dangerous working life was in an interlude, like the ones I went to Mexico for, while Mexican migrants wove other nets, now including me. A series of signs and objects marked the connections.

Lucas Lorenzo, Danza de los Tigres, Xalitla, Guerrero, 2010. Acrylic paint on masonite with clear lacquer, 12 × 16 in. Private collection.

CHAPTER SIX

The Magic Mountain

Chiapas, September 1996

WHEN JANET SAID, "This has been going on long enough," Marcey's eighty-fifth birthday party had been in full swing for two weeks. It coincided with the opening at La Galeria of her show "*La flor de México son los ancianos*," an exhibition of photographs of old people, to which whole families came to see their old person. Anthropologist Joan, of the duraznos fame, was there from California, and their friend Carmelita had come from Oregon.

Standing in the street outside Marcey's house at six in the morning, I saw for the first time the typical crepe paper screen woven over the door for these occasions. Her friends were there, and the mariachi band started up. Marcey opened the door from the inside and stepped through the crepe paper into the street, reenacting her birth. It was unexpectedly moving. Susanna Ekholm-Miller, an anthropologist and the local maker of paper crowns, put one on Marcey's white-haired head. We then went inside and ate tamales and drank hot chocolate. After that, we went down to the zocalo for a brunch at Hotel Santa Clara, and Janet explained to me the glories of *huevos motuleños*: fried eggs, tortillas, black beans, cheese, bananas, and peas. Janet and

Marcey's house was a salon for the English-speaking expat community. As Jan de Vos, an ex-Jesuit who left the church because it would not ordain Maya priests, told me, "They worked in the morning and then opened the house in the afternoon. We came for the conversation, but also for the cookies."

A banquet followed at dinnertime at Kiki and Gabriel's hotel. Seating was royal. I ended up next to Doctor David Halpern, a Boston surgeon turned Chiapas social scientist, who mentioned that all indigenous men beat their wives. "'How else do you correct them?' they say."

"All women need to have guns," I responded. Everyone gave me a shocked look. I was under the influence of the railroad, but I didn't see why that wouldn't solve the problem. As it turned out, the Zapatistas did just that.

After two weeks of conversation and sending out for pizza, Janet pulled the plug. Since Carmelita had never been to Guatemala, we decided to go, and Janet and Marcey drove us to the border, of course stopping in Teopisca for pork ribs. My dilemma of where to take Carmelita was solved when we learned that the festival of the Virgin of the Rosary was going to take place in Quetzaltenango, where we were staying. We simply sat in the town square while Maya disembarked from buses, each group wearing their traditional dress, the colors every imaginable combination of hue, texture, thread, and design. A contingent of metallic-blue-skirted women from Lake Atitlán passed by us, their orchid huipils adorned with bright pink flowers. Around their hair they wore turbans of narrow woven silk embroidered with animals, flowers, and geometric designs. Around their shoulders they wore lapis and fuchsia rebozos, tied with shocking-pink yarn dangle balls.

"Wow," Carmelita commented, lapsing into hippie speak.

"Far out" was all I could manage. "Look."

The next group off the bus were the rainbow people, the women's wrapped skirts horizontally striped in every prismatic hue, their huipils likewise banded but vertically, their rebozos echoing their skirts, their head cloths repeating their huipils. They were moving prisms, light catching moisture, fire and water combining to create motion, as in the creation myth of the Fifth World. Later, in the color relief of night, we paused outside the church in the throng of people listening to the Virgin's service. Beside us, the Maya church guilds waited to proceed into the church and up the nave. By the flames of their candles and the electric Christmas lights strung on the carnival booths nearby, I could see long, ceremonial yellow-and-black huipils, bright chrome-yellow silk wound head scarves on the women and, on the men, long black wool Spanish capes lined with glowing crimson silk. In baskets on their heads, the women carried the largest vegetables I had ever seen. Their colors glowed orange, white, red, and green. All at once an oboe sounded, and the guild ran forward into the church.

The following week, I settled into my seat on the Primera Plus bus from Mexico City's Terminal Norte to Guanajuato. I looked into the plastic bag the attendant had handed me when I got on and discarded the white bread and ham sandwich. I drank the orange juice. I felt I needed it. Carmelita had sneezed on me in Guatemala. The ferocity of the virus amazed me. It would do anything to live. Now, traveling alone, I was transporting it. I was reading Thomas Mann's *The Magic Mountain*, and his hero was getting all too comfortable in the Swiss tuberculosis sanitarium. I suspected he would never leave. My throat felt like raw meat, and the suitcase I could manage when well would take me to the bottom now as I hauled it from cab to hotel, looking for nonallergenic tile floors, sniffing out moldy carpets. I was near to San Miguel de

Allende, and I made a dash for its comfort, its gringo-ness. I found an old hotel near the market, only foreigners staying there, with color TV, a pool, and a dining room. In bed, shaking, I piled on the blankets.

Mann's hero was going for his lung X-ray, although he was just a visitor. "Flee," I whispered. "Run."

In the morning, the breakfast room was like a Protestant church. No one acknowledged my entrance, the only sounds a tinkle of spoon on glass, the shuffle of newsprint. Mann's European characters peered back at me from over their teacups and buns. No one would meet my eye.

Finally, a photographer from Mexico City, Hans Stoppelman, joined my table.

"The reason I live here," he confided, "is my passion for young girls. In Mexico, they admire you for this."

He gave me his card. Later that day, still feverish, I fled San Miguel, tossing *The Magic Mountain* into a handy trash bin. I wasn't tough enough for German lit.

Ricardo de la Loma, Espíritu Tomate, San Pablito, Puebla, 1997. Amate paper cutout, 7.5 × 5.5 in. Private collection.

CHAPTER SEVEN

The Spirit of the Tomato

San Pablito, Puebla, April 1997

APRIL 7, 1997, I flew to Mexico City with Lynn Marsh, an artist who made bronze Green Man figures and drew a figure she named the Great Tomato Diva in pastel. Lynn was managing events for Printer's Inc. Bookstore in Palo Alto when I came there to read. I got the feeling she was captivated by my persona in *Boomer: Railroad Memoirs,* but after breast cancer and physical trouble coming back to work on the railroad, I didn't feel like that person anymore. I was working in the San Jose yard as a switchman so I could be close to home in Santa Cruz and sleep nights. I knew that I had to do something about my railroad job, but I needed the health insurance, and I was afraid to leave my docs. The five-year waiting period for recurrence was a bad dream.

Lynn lived the artist's life. Her rented converted garage in Menlo Park was filled with worktables. Her TV had a weaving from San Andrés Larráinzar, Chiapas, covering the screen. She made paper from lichen and mushrooms, scouted the upscale groceries for spices, and rented space in a foundry in the warehouse district that I worked in every day on my switching job.

77

"I want to rescue the tomatoes," Lynn said. "They shouldn't taste like cardboard."

Her diva looked like she tasted succulent. Her large, plump bottom and mountainous knees reclined in a valley with steep, green, knee-like mountains, lit by sunlight making its way between cumulus clouds.

"You know," I said, "there's a place in Mexico where they revere the spirit of the tomato plant. I saw one of their bark-paper cutouts in the FONART store in Mexico City. We could go there."

Lynn had an artist friend in Mexico City who had met her Mexican husband on a vacation to Acapulco thirty years before. Betty had lunch with us and gave us a tip about a photography library in Pachuca where her friend Gina worked. It was on our way, sort of. Lynn brightened up at the mention of library, as she was a former librarian and loved citations. You could get reproductions of anything in their collection, which was most famous for the photographer Agustín Casasola's work. Pachuca was the place the green obsidian came from and was also famous for pastis, Welsh miners' cakes, and ixtle weaving from the fiber of the maguey cactus, which grew in the nearby Mexquital Valley. The people who lived in San Pablito, the Otomí, also made this their home.

They were ancient producers of paper, although San Pablito was one of the few remaining locations that produced it now. The paper came from stripping the bark from the fig tree and felting it into sheets. The thousands of ancient codices destroyed by the Spanish were made of bark paper, as were ceremonial clothing, offerings to the gods, and, in San Pablito and other nearby towns, cutout figures for ritual uses. These were what had caught my eye in FONART.

I had cutouts of the seed spirits of the peanut, pineapple, long bean, chile, and banana. Of the attack spirits, I had Lord Nagual, Moctezuma, the Queen of the Bad Earth, the President of Hell, the Bull Snout That Does Not Respect Parents, Lord Devil, Lord Jew, the Bad Siren, and the Lord of the Night. Of the spirits of the mountain, I had the little bird with infants in its wings and the eagle with four heads, also holding infants. These birds work with the Lord of the Mountain as helpers. I also had four sacred books, made almanac-style out of bark paper, describing curing rituals: *A History of a Nagual Sorcerer of San Pablito*; *A History of an Offering to Saint Tecuil, the Hearth Spirit*; *A History of an Ancient Curing*; and *An Offering to Ask for Rain*. These books were authored by Alfonso García Tellez, a shaman still living there.

Lynn and I rode the bus to Pachuca, about two hours north of Mexico City, at the base of the mountains. Gina took us to the Fototeca Nacional, a glass and steel building with computerized catalogs. It was easy to get prints from their collection, and Lynn ordered a print of an Otomí woman from the 1920s, made from a glass photographic plate. In the folk art museum I saw an ixtle tablecloth for twelve that reminded me of my grandmother's heirloom crochet. In the morning we boarded a bus to Tulancingo, where we would look for a transfer.

In the cavernous bus station, as we were talking about San Pablito, a man behind us overheard.

"For San Pablito, you take the bus to Pahuatlán. Then take a taxi. You are North Americans? I worked in LA. What do you think about Proposition 187?"

"Well," I said, "we're against it, or we wouldn't be here, taking buses."

His advice was good, and we found the right kiosk. An hour later we got off in Pahuatlán, a town cradled above a misty ravine, surrounded by clouds. It smelled wet, with a chill in the air.

"Good hotel?" I asked a man at the Tres Estrellas de Oro bus ticket counter.

"Hotel San Carlos," he said, giving directions.

The hotel was grand—a red tile roof, banana trees, bougainvillea spilling over white walls, on an overlook of the Pahuatilta River canyon. I was picky about the room, until we got the corner at the far end of the hotel with views on two sides of the canyon. Lynn opened the windows to let in the humid breeze. I collapsed on my bed. I had gotten us here. San Pablito was across the canyon, and in the morning we could take a cab there. Meanwhile, we set out to explore the village. Laden mules traversed the stone streets. There was one other hotel, clean but basic.

Graffiti on the walls had to do with voting. "*Apúntate y ponte al día. ¡Tu credencial para votar!*" Sign up and get up-to-date with your voting credential!

An artist's studio, belonging to Rafael Lechuga, advertised paintings specializing in amate, or bark, paper. We went in and met Rafael. Lynn wanted to get down to metaphysics quickly, and I was the translator.

"Do you believe in God?" This seemed way too personal at this stage, but I tried my best. They were hugging at the end of a half hour.

Another conversation we had was with a woman who called paper cutting "*brujería*," or witchcraft, and asked us if we believed in it. Clearly, she thought that we didn't and that for tourists to encourage such backwardness was irresponsible. In such situations my Spanish was not up to explaining the complexities of politically correct acceptance of other people's customs. But she did make me think. I was much more accepting of foreign religions, particularly indigenous ones, than I was of religious fundamentalism I was more familiar with. "Why is that?" I wondered.

Maybe if I had grown up seeing chicken blood spattered on paper cutouts I would feel the way she did.

We ate something delicious called *chacales* in brandy sauce at the hotel restaurant. They were crawfish from the river. A young couple a few seats away offered to join our table. We thought, "Why not?"

"What are you doing here, at such a nontourist spot?" He was charming, she was attractive. We chatted for an hour, and they offered to show us around the next day.

"We pick you up at 9:00 a.m.?" They assured us, "Don't worry about your bill."

"*Muy amable*," very kind, we thought. Then, as the waiter chased us down in the lobby, "Not so amable."

"*No, señora, ellos no pagaron a su cuenta.*" No, they didn't pay your bill.

Probably no 9:00 a.m. pickup either, I foretold. Kind of made you wonder what other fantasies they had.

We got a cab in the morning for San Pablito. Not a bad dirt road, and the cliffhanging village of cinder-block houses seemed moderately prosperous. A few questions in the square led us to the house of Ricardo de la Loma, a paper cutter and maker. Amate fiber was boiling in a large pot in the corner, and strips hung from the rafters. The *tablas*, or wooden boards, and the metates, or flat stones, for pounding the paper were outside, and the windows and doors were open, with children, animals, and the elderly walking in and out.

Ricardo said he was one of a few cutters in the village who followed the old traditions of ceremonial designs. He only wanted to make us the positive side of the pantheon: seed and mountain spirits and sun designs. We watched as he folded the brown amate and with scissors made one continuous, flowing cut. He cut for me the spirits of the *jitomate*, *tomate*, Señor del Monte, Santa Rosa, marijuana, and guava. He also cut two small sun sign pictures with peanuts and guavas and two large sun sign pictures with horses and chiles. These were mounted on a backdrop of white amate, which was translucent with light behind it.

"Son sombras, decimos," he told me. We call them shadows.

Ricardo knew the author of the folding amate books, don Alfonso García, and he guided us to his house, where he also had a roasted-chicken business. Don Alfonso signed my books with obvious pleasure, and he also cut two seed spirits for me of chile and pineapple. Meanwhile, San Pablito was preparing for a fiesta, and people were raising a blue plastic tent in the area in front of the church. A fireworks bull was resting on the church steps. It was raining off and on, and clouds hovered on the green mountains. Just like the ones in Lynn's Great Tomato Diva pastel.

Ricardo had asked us to give a lift to two friends of his, Kerin, an American, and Carlos, a Cuban, who needed a ride out of town. We met them at the new cultural center, a cooperative where artists could sell their work. They seemed a little anxious, and Kerin told us that San Pablito politics had made it uncomfortable, dangerous even, for Carlos to stay in town. They had been working for the cultural center. We dropped them off in Pahuatlán and came back to the Hotel San Carlos. It was late afternoon. We both had chacales on our minds.

"I'll pay for dinner," Lynn said. "I found this!" She placed a thousand-peso banknote on the table. "It's a hundred dollars."

Mexico had recently devalued its currency, and some enterprising person had passed the now worthless note to Lynn as change. Mexican banks were ruthless about even slightly torn money.

The part of the artist's life that had always scared me was the money part. I had both fists around my railroad paycheck, and I felt caught in a monkey trap. Now that, because of my history with cancer, I couldn't even buy health insurance on my own—assuming I could even pay for it—I felt doubly trapped. Could I live the way Lynn did, with her grace?

"No problem," I said after she realized the banknote was worthless. "We can spend a dollar and have a fine dinner. We don't need chacales at the San Carlos."

In fact, for about a buck, we happily ate *enfrijoladas,* a black bean paste over handmade corn tortillas with a garnish of fresh cheese and onions, in a small, clean restaurant overlooking the town.

The full moon was rising behind us as we descended to our hotel. We had some *zapotes negros,* a black custardy fruit, from the market, and Lynn incorporated them into a watercolor on amate paper while I made notes on the day. Across the canyon we could hear the fireworks from San Pablito's fiesta.

Before dawn, I was somewhere in a dream when I felt compelled to open my eyes. Glowing on the opposite wall was a seed spirit cutout in a frame. It was a tree with thorns on its trunk. *Dios espinoso.* I lay frozen in my bed. After a few minutes, the image faded and did not reappear. I went to the door and opened it. No one was in the moonlit corridor.

Two years earlier, before I went back to the railroad after chemotherapy, I had visited a shaman in Santa Fe, New Mexico. He worked for Blue Sky soft drinks and did healing for free. His office was lined with silver-and-blue cans, and he did a kind of Reiki energy treatment while hovering over my body.

"I don't find any cancer here," he said. "You can go back to work. Drink water."

Later that night in Santa Fe, I had a vivid dream of a beaded staff in the desert.

In the San Carlos, when the sun warmed us, we woke up. First thing, I went into the corridor. Birds were singing. The maid was pushing her cart. I noticed a window into our room from the hall that I had not remembered, and directly in front of it, growing through an opening in the stairwell, was a young ceiba tree, with a green, thorny trunk. The full moon must have cast the shadow through the small window, framing it upon the wall opposite in our room.

"We call them shadows," Ricardo had said.

The ceiba, with its red roots growing down to the waters below earth and its symmetrical umbrella of leaves reaching into the clouds, is an ancient symbol of the Tree of Life, spanning all three worlds: the underworld, the surface of the earth, and the sky.

Lynn flew home from Mexico City before I did. I was both sad and relieved. Translating was wearing me down, since in Mexico, everyone is playing music at all times.

"What are they saying in that song?"

"He's like a fish, and he wants to bump his nose against her fish tank and spend the night in it all wet."

But I did meet Betty again, Lynn's friend who had given us the tip about the Fototeca, and her husband, Pepe, who worked as a biologist for conservation projects in the rain forest. After dinner in the Zona Rosa, as they were saying good-bye, he opened the trunk of the car to get a sweater. It was full of butterfly art.

"We try to get them to do this," Pepe said, "instead of cutting down the trees, but it's a hard sell."

Former worm, wink of iridescent wing in streetlamp light. Mexico, *un cajón de sorpresas*. A drawer of surprises.

Altar, Oaxaca de Juárez, Oaxaca, 1997. Papier-mâché, 12 × 4 × 4 in. Private collection.

The Day of the Dead

Oaxaca City, October 1997

SUMMER OF HELL on the railroad: the year after the Union
Pacific merger that had all traffic on the southern lines frozen in
place while the chief of the Federal Railroad Administration,
Jolene Molitoris, sent us a videotape in which she told us, "I know
you're tired." Not the half of it, Jolene. But I had a place of refuge
for ten days, a little room whose twenty-foot door opened to the
tropical stars and where I could hear Lupita say, "Good morning,
Beautiful—more beans?" I waited for my Spanish-speaking persona to emerge, one much sweeter than my own. My visits to Oaxaca were chances to inhabit this person again, as easily as opening
the glass and iron doors that fronted on García Vigil Street and
sitting down on the red velvet sofa that smelled of Gaspar.

Oaxaca at this time of year was a major tourist destination, and
local travel agencies, Spanish-language schools, and art galleries
offer tours of pueblo graveyards on the Catholic four days of the
Day of the Dead celebration. I met many other North Americans
who were going here or there, but I decided to stay with my family
and accompany them. During the week I noticed skeletons in
tutus appearing on cantina doors and Halloween masks on sale in

the market and in the zocalo. Some Oaxacans disapproved of the Halloween masks—this year Bill Clinton and Monica Lewinsky masks were big, along with Mexico's ex-president, Carlos Salinas de Gortari—as diluting to their own traditions. The opportunity for candy from the tourists, however, made the syncretism inevitable for the street children. In the market about four days before the fiesta, the altar-making necessities began to arrive. An entire street was devoted to them and filled up with truckloads of orange and red marigolds. The city smelled of copal—the sap of the ceiba tree, used as sacred incense by the indigenous religions. Women sold *pan de muerto*—sweet bread baked in the shape of people, with sugar faces. There were carts specializing in sugar skulls filled with anise water, as well as papier-mâché or clay skeletons engaged in every conceivable human activity.

I bought the skeleton nurse, the hatted woman called Catrina, several brazen hussies, a hairdresser, and a woman in a bathtub. I bit into a sugar skull, and the acrid anise nauseated me and stained my fingers bright pink. I discarded the pieces on a cardboard carton, from which they were immediately seized and eaten by two little girls. I moved along to another aisle, where they were selling cut paper in all colors to lay down as a bed on the home altars. I bought pink-and-black cutout Catrinas, then miniature dishes for the sticks of chocolate and the mole, and a seven-ingredient paste for chicken stew. I bought plastic Dracula fangs and dangling rearview-mirror skeletons. I bought a papier-mâché altar with a skull and candles, painted deep blue. I bought copal and a little dish to burn it in and charcoal bits to keep it glowing. I bought marigolds, and tuberose for its room-filling smell, and pan de muerto, and a cab to carry it all back home.

To my surprise, Elda was making an altar in their courtyard. The family was very proud of their Spanish descent, and I wasn't sure if they would follow this indigenous tradition or not. She was also burning copal. When I asked about the copal, she told me that "the dead like it." A picture of her Spanish father, Lupita's husband, rested on the altar along with a picture of La Virgen de la Soledad. Elda's altar had mescal on it, along with cigarettes and chocolate. All things she likes as well. We all sat down in the courtyard before dinner, and she and Lupita had a glass of mescal and a cigarette. There were definite fringe benefits of providing a feast for the dead—they partook only of the essence, not of the food itself.

After dinner, we got in the Volkswagen and set off for the municipal graveyard to clean off the family graves. Parking was a problem, since most of the city was here doing the same thing. A circus had set up in front of the graveyard, a conjunction I had seen in Day of the Dead art but thought was metaphor. In Mexico often life trumped metaphor. Picking our way through the carnival dinosaurs, we entered the municipal graveyard through the galleries that contain niches for cremated remains. This was the space set aside for altars competing for awards, and the entire graveyard was circled by them. At the center of the space was a community altar for the unknown dead, decorated elaborately with pan de muerto, a marigold-encrusted straw arch, tropical fruit and other food, greenery, mescal, and other goodies. A carpet made of marigold flowers formed a pathway to the altar. In the four corners surrounding it, other flower carpet "paintings" had been created—a traditional part of the indigenous ceremony of mourning.

Our purpose today was to clean off Lupita's husband's grave, which actually resembled a motel room, complete with sliding glass door and desiccated flowers left over from last year's Day of the Dead. Elda put down the fresh flowers we brought on a neighboring grave while she swept out the room. Lupita and I watched the unfolding scene as other families swept, ate, and chatted with the deceased—reminding them that now they had new family members, filling them in on gossip. In our fascination we failed to notice that someone stole our flowers, and Elda had to go buy more from the vendors at the gates.

"*Sinvergüenzas*," Lupita exclaimed, but without much surprise. At eighty-two she had witnessed a considerable slide in community morals.

At the cemetery I told Lupita that we have nothing like the Day of the Dead and that graveyards are rarely visited.

"Death must be very sad in the United States," she said.

Elda was much more upset—so much so that in leaving she could not find the Volkswagen and was convinced that it, too, had been purloined. I didn't think so and waited with Lupita as Elda searched the streets surrounding the cemetery. Finally we hired a taxi to take us around until we found it.

Back at the casa, I assembled my altar, thinking about my friend Josie Cole, who had died in February of the previous year. I put down the Dracula plastic fangs and borrowed a cigarette from Elda to place in the mouth. This did not strike me as at all macabre. It reminded me of how it felt to spend time with Josie. When you stoop down to enter that low door to be with someone close to death, life seems precious, magical, and even funny.

I poured a full shot of mescal for the altar—the next morning the glass was half-full because of evaporation. Later, wandering in the market, I saw that the marigolds and skulls and bread of the dead were gone, and another day, with its own particular nature and necessities, had arrived.

Ramona Zapatista Doll, San Cristóbal de las Casas, Chiapas, 1994.
Wool, 9 × 3 × 2.5 in. Private collection.

Hermanas, Sisters

Chiapas, February 1999

I WENT TO see Marcey in February, for the first time since Janet's death three months before. Janet had died in a taxi on her way to Tuxtla Gutiérrez before Marcey could get her to the Methodist hospital in Houston for one more rescue, one more passover. Marcey felt she had failed in her job of saving Janet by putting her in the cab to die in transit.

In Marcey's pocket, folded in a white cloth, was half of a million-year-old fossilized shell, a spiral of stone. In the morning, I found her curled up like the shell in the sun window, sleeping with her cat, Luli. Janet's headstone in white marble was in the garden under a tree. At the base of the stone was the other half of the fossilized shell. Marcey was trying to communicate with her through the Ouija board and baffled that she wasn't receiving any messages. She was also reading Janet's diaries—not the best pursuit for peace of mind. The Ouija board had a lot of explaining to do.

Marcey was working on her photography book, *The Burden of Time*, which spanned fifty years of images, from Maya villages to street scenes in San Cristóbal. I had urged her to compile it and had put her together with Stanford University Press, who had produced a book of mine. I thought it was great timing that she had something to do other than engage in the outrage of lost communication.

"A hundred images," she said. "I haven't made a hundred good images in my lifetime. And who am I to put my work out there?"

Humility and self-criticism were Marcey's way of being. Her photographs always expressed a relationship. The spark of communication was always there: in the boy reading *El Globo*, looking down yet acknowledging the photographer with his secret smile; in the challenge in the eye of doña Pava, claiming all the space on the street, particularly the space taken by the photographer. Marcey's first question, upon seeing me, always was "And what are you doing?"

Which she asked me as soon as I arrived. I was staying at her house for the first time, sleeping in her room while she slept in Janet's. I had just interviewed for a new job, a life changer. With my second book now out, I had gotten interviews from two universities to teach creative writing and could leave the railroad behind. While I was at Marcey's, I got the offer from Kennesaw State University in Georgia, and I said yes.

One day we drove out to Amatenango del Valle to visit an old friend of hers, Juliana López, the potter who had put the artistry of the town on the map. I noticed that Marcey was wearing two watches, set to the same time. The turnoff on the road to the Guatemalan border was marked by pottery birds on the side of the road and smoke from the wood kilns floating in the humid air. The trip was for me, but also it was part of Marcey's process of going out alone, no longer part of a couple, and receiving the condolences for Janet, something that she would do gradually, as she felt up to it. Marcey was still driving her Tsuru, a car kept in order by the "maestro," a mechanic as old as Marcey. Now at eighty-eight years old, sometimes she would ask me to drive home at night, but I often felt the power of her spirit behind the wheel, still strong and attractive.

We were greeted by a white-braided woman who was chasing ducks out of her yard. Juliana looked like she could still throw pots. Her house was comfortable but spare, and she pulled chairs around in a circle and invited us to have tea. After introductions, they talked about work and Juliana's children, politics, and the world now. Juliana finally said, "Since Janet is gone, will you marry?"

I realized that I knew very little about the world here, how deeply traditional it was. Marcey and Janet were in the *hermanas* slot—sisters. An accepted way to live, but now what?

"I don't wish to be ordered around in my own house," Marcey said.

"But what will happen to the house when you die?" she asked.

"They will sell it," Marcey said.

Juliana nodded, passed the tea.

"They never give up, do they?" I said when we were in the car.

The next day she took me to the places she was photographing for her show *Adiós Jovel*. Fifty years' difference, the same time of day, the same location.

"Look," she said, holding the original photograph. "Do you see it then?"

Chiapas, Christmas 1999

At Christmas during my first year in Georgia, I visited Marcey again, and we went to Zinacantán, where they were celebrating a fiesta involving a bull and male actors dressed as grandmothers and grandfathers who were engaged in lots of obscene joking. We sat in the small chapel where the men involved in the ritual entered, did things, and left. Green pine needles covered the floor, tables of lit candles fronted the flower-covered altars. The officials were at the central table drinking. We were all sitting around the room on benches when it occurred to me that Marcey and I were the only women there.

"Except for him," Marcey said, pointing out the man dressed as a grandmother and riding a stick horse.

I later read about the fiesta. The grandmothers were mocking women who acted like men. That would be us.

Marcey's friend Gayle Walker, a photographer and painter, had an exhibition in the Museo de las Culturas Populares, and we went. I had given Marcey a rainbow beaded necklace that I had bought in the market and kept one for myself. When Gayle saw us wearing them, she commented how beautiful they were.

"We are the gay parade," Marcey said.

Mexico City, December 2000

The following year, when all the digital clocks were supposed to deconstruct, I was in Acapulco with my friends Carter and Tom for Christmas. We got the news that Marcey had fallen, but we didn't know any details. I had to fly home from Mexico City, and I arrived three hours early at the airport for my flight, waiting while Aeroméxico inspected every bag in the line for bombs and then attached a little tag that was supposed to verify there was no trace of explosives. They were very methodical, very slow. I wished I had stopped for breakfast, then lunch. Still not up to the counter, twenty minutes to boarding, there was a flurry of activity, then a new line opened and a rush to fill it. He who was first was now last, and so I, along with thirty others, was squeezed out. Only a year away from the railroad, I still had judgments about transportation procedures. This was a fucking mess. Women sitting on their suitcases burst into tears. Old people had tragic expressions. Who knows what occasions were being missed? I joined the compensation line, even pounded on the desk, which probably gave the impeccably dressed staff some feelings of superiority. They had to get them from somewhere.

"The next available flight is in two days," they said. "Here is your hotel voucher."

It was really worrying about Marcey that had me upset. My cat wouldn't miss me. I had no place to go, really. They took us to the crew's hotel, the Riazor, in a dicey neighborhood near the airport. At dinner, I spotted a lesbian couple I had seen in our ticket line. They too had been bumped. They invited me over. Gaydar. Gloria was from Mexico, and her girlfriend was from Georgia. They were there visiting Gloria's family. Would I join them tomorrow, as the family was coming to the rescue? Of course.

Her uncle, aunt, and two cousins arrived the next morning and escorted us via Metro to the Basílica of Our Lady of Guadalupe. No, they would not let us pay for the Metro tickets or anything else, for that matter. We got off at La Villa–Basílica, the closest stop. Since it was December, many pilgrims were navigating the blocks leading up to the church on their knees, some with eternal flames or banners announcing their hometowns. Gloria's uncle was a Mexican-history buff, and he was very happy to have someone to talk with. I was trying out my reading on him.

"There were many revolutionary appearances," I said, "of the Virgin to the Indians. She wanted to help them throw out the Spanish."

"She was revolutionary," he responded, "only in the revolution, when Father Hidalgo raised the banner."

We got on the moving belt that enabled visitors to pass beneath the image of the Virgin on the mantle of Juan Diego. This was the miraculous image that proved her appearance in 1531 to this peasant. Perhaps the collective belief made the feelings appear, but there was something there, some vibration.

We took the train back to the family's house for an elaborate dinner, and the uncle showed me his bookcase. Later they escorted us back to our hotel. Of course we could not pay for the Metro.

Later still, I found out Marcey had broken her hip, but it only slowed her down a little. She had tripped on a rug on her porch and was horizontal for a while.

"It was interesting," she said. "It felt like I was flying."

Beaded Snake, Huichol/Wixárika, Zapopan, Jalisco, 1995. Glass beads, bees-
wax, wood, 7 × 15 × 6 in. Private collection.

Real de Catorce

Real de Catorce, San Luis Potosí, April 2002

IN APRIL I flew to León, Mexico, on my spring break. I was in my third year teaching in Georgia, and I had just resigned from the railroad after a two-year leave, which I had taken when I was unsure of the change. I felt sad to see that part of my life gone now, although the railroad is never gone. It is its own country, a long, thin country extending everywhere.

León was famous for shoes. The bus from the airport was full of shoe store owners on buying trips, the station surrounded by factory outlets in concentric rings, the malls full of shoes in retail settings.

"Hey, *patrona*," salesmen saluted me, assuming I was a store owner. In the lesser flea markets, the boys were ruder, called me "señor."

León made all kinds of shoes, but mainly cowboy couture. Cowboy boots of exotic skins, cowboy belts, leather jackets, quillwork, fringe, motorcycle leathers, duffels, bags. Cowboy gear, bridles, saddles, holsters, whips. Mariachi boots in every color and texture—fuzzies, baby blue suede; bathtubs full of mariachi boots. I bought a white hair-on pair after looking all day. And a black fringe jacket with quillwork and beads. A beaded buckskin vest and leather sneakers. Back to the Holiday Inn for a nap.

Evening on the street, I was still not fully present, still in transit, the trappings of the university, Georgia, and my underlying discontent shedding off me in patches; I was grumpy from travel, passing people like a ghost. I lurched into a movie theater playing *Silence of the Lambs*, descended down a ramp and down three floors into a basement space crudely partitioned to house four screens. I squeezed into an aisle, the room already dark, the floor some black plastic sticky foam, trying not to stumble in my new León sneakers. My feet slid as in some ice rink surface under the seats, wet, black, slick like sex lube, Astroglide slick. I looked around. Nobody else thought it strange to have a wet, slick floor in the movies. In the surreal, Mexico does not disappoint.

Bus from León to San Luis Potosí, up the Bajío. The third day I lost the grumbles, started to blend, to smile, to let color, the dry air, the blue dome of church and sky, nopal and agave, Joshua tree sink in. I had been missing the landscape of the West. Beside the road, quarries for porous pink stone. I was unreadable to people here, my Spanish unintelligible as I started to speak it again, and I was not yet laughing at myself. I wheeled my suitcase from taxi to hotel in the old city center—stone hotel, wrought iron balcony, high ceilings, formal deskman. Walking out into the plaza, I saw few Indians on the streets, mainly Triques from Oaxaca selling weaving and wearing their red-and-white striped huipils. Not much *fayuca*, untaxed merchandise, either, just families walking, everybody eating snow cones, candied nuts, corn on the cob, watching clowns. I missed this in Marietta, Georgia, being able to go out at night and take pleasure in the company of fellow citizens; having a center bounded by churches that are open continuously on Sunday, people coming and going, walking, sitting, old and young. I had almost slowed down enough to join in the pleasure of everyday life. What did I have if I didn't have this?

Orange, fuchsia, and crimson bougainvillea fronted a cobalt blue wall. An interior showed folkloric masks mounted on a yellow canvas. The dry air of the altiplano, the bare rock mountains, the total nudity of the land made any color vivid with light. The warm brown skin of the people made any color come alive.

On the bus to the Balneario de Gogorrón, the hot springs, I met Ana, a dentist who had her office in Bledos, where her father, mother, and three brothers were born. She and her two sisters were born in San Luis. "*Tu tienes casa en Bledos,*" you have a house in Bledos, she told me. I believed her.

Silk ikat rebozos are the most admired craft objects of the state, fabled to be fine enough to be pulled through a ring. Near the hot springs was the town of the workshops, Santa María del Río. I took a taxi there, and my driver, like every taxi driver, had worked in the United States. When migrants return, they have the skill to talk to foreigners. He told me his cousin owned El Palenque restaurant in Atlanta. He said since the Kansas City Southern bought the railroad here, they haven't had passenger service north and south. This is what the US railroads always want—to fire half the workforce and get rid of passenger service. I had heard the railroad stopped at Estación Catorce, the sacred peyote grounds of the Huichol, or Wixárika, people, but apparently no more. I had read about and seen a film of their annual pilgrimage from the western sierra to the desert here to gather peyote, how they continue to make it despite highways, fences, and the modern world rushing by them. Ptolemy Tompkins in *This Tree Grows Out of Hell: Mesoamerica and the Search for the Magical Body* names them as a successful shamanistic society who through isolation held onto their world view, unlike the more imperial Mesoamericans. Looking at a map of the railroad tracks, I had felt a secret thrill that I might be able to disembark in the middle of Wirikuta, where the Wixárika ran backward and spoke backward in order to disassemble the normal and enter into the sacred.

In Santa María, rebozos were for sale everywhere. It was the León of rebozos. These long, thin shawls are the defining object of femininity in Mexico. They are a cross between the practical indigenous cloths used for carrying babies, covering the head, and wrapping up mother and child against the cold and the Spanish silk shawls embroidered with roses and fringe imported from Manila. Their length makes them unique. I bought one that measured 106 inches, and a full 20 inches of that was fringe. The color pattern was called *caramelo*, and it was red, gold, pale lavender, dark green, indigo, and orange, with black crochet fringe. Each rebozo came with its own inlaid cedar box. It cost me $400. "No rebozo is worth $400," Marcey said to me later on the phone. Their looms were long and thin also, with the dyed silk thread drying on lines hung around the walls. The weaving was done by hand in the style of backstrap weaving, using a piece of wood. The weaver demonstrated the claim to fineness, pulling a completed rebozo through a silver ring. Lesser rebozos were made of *arracele*, a rayon thread, but they would not pull through a ring. Nor would the fine ones of cotton ikat. The longer the crochet and fringe, the finer the rebozo.

In San Luis I made friends with the female tourist police, who were universally good looking and wore cream-colored uniforms. They loaded me up with posters and brochures for Real de Catorce, a ghost town three hours north. On the highway getting there, I saw ocotillo roadside stands where rattlesnake skins hung drying in the air. "Sorcerers," Leslie Marmon Silko told me when she heard about it later. Real de Catorce was a silver mining town, once the richest in Mexico and now the site of an annual October pilgrimage to the church dedicated to Saint Francis. I changed buses in Matehuala and then entered the town through a one-way tunnel in the rock, formerly for railroad tracks. Little boys met me, offering to guide me. The place smelled of money; Hollywood had just left after making *The Mexican* with Brad Pitt and Julia Roberts. Dark Swiss hotels harbored leering druggie guests. Steering my roller luggage over the cobblestones, I found Hotel San Juan, a five-dollar *pensión* the owner was busy painting while playing norteño music. My room had a cane ceiling, too dry to rot. The town overlooked the desert where the Kansas City Southern now ran freights, where Estación Catorce was abandoned, and where peyote lived. Where the railroad ran I was home.

Southeastern color is diffuse, a wall of green, the open car window invaded by wisteria perfume, palpable air, azaleas floating in a light-eating chlorophyll bowl, distance obliterated. Here the color, paint splashed over a paint-can planter, oxidized in days, and became desertified. The rough wood doors, framed by whitewashed adobe, were painted the blue of the river that flows through Havasu Canyon in the Grand Canyon. A maguey cactus in bloom, pale-butter petal cascade. Pink soul flowers, quadratic with a cream center. Datura, here called *dos de abril*, opened its poison bell. Fuzzy yellow cholla fingers, little tight pink buds on a fruit tree in the church garden. Sere spring, cautious. A north wind, low pressure, blowing the windows shut. This air was familiar to me, being from Los Angeles—another desert connected to this one. Tomorrow I would ride horses with a boy guide.

I had read Konrad Theodor Preuss, a German ethnologist who studied the Wixárika culture; according to Preuss, to the Wixárika deer were stars killed by the sun each day with help from the morning star, Kayumari. The ritual peyote hunt was before the rainy season, when the sun pushed back the night and approached the solstice; the hunt brought rain and watered the corn.

I woke to deer stars fading as the rising sun cast finger shadows over Wirikuta.

As a brakeman, when I worked in the north of this desert, I could see what I wanted to in the landscape passing by. As if I were reading a book, it was my thoughts I passed in guise of the rock paintings of the moving light. Histories are like journeys from a moving train—there is a fixed point of view, the shadowed reader safe in her bed, the book always open to the next page.

I now lived in a new paradigm, in the American South, a college teacher with a respectable address, although the CSX mainline ran just behind my house, and it signified choice: until this spring, at any time I could return. As a quixotic gesture, I wrote a note along with my failure to report for duty. No one answered. The railroad is an invasive vein connecting all places, but it let me live outside and see the plants and animals, see the night sky without light pollution, drink the different times of day and night. This placed me in kinship with people who lived and worked outside. I was losing that in Georgia. My work was inside, and the outside was a wall of breathing green, like the inside of a cow.

Real de Catorce reminded me of the choice and of the change in the work that led to it.

"*Trabajo nos lleva*," an artist at Alejandro Santiago's art farm in Oaxaca once told me. Work carries us. Santiago cast 2,500 migrants in high-fired clay to replace the migrants who left his native village. "I miss them," he said.

The Oaxacan anthem, "Canción mixteca," tells the story of migrants thinking of their lost home so much that they feel they will die of their sentiments. The machines of the world that demand our work, that eat our lives, had been here before. The Santa Ana mine, richest in Mexico, had created the town. The pressure of being enslaved by Spaniards to work in the mines sent the Wixárika west, to the refuge of the sierra, where the basis for their sustenance transformed into corn farming. Peyote became the road home, the medicine that could bring the desert to them and, with the deer blood, saturate their present land with the spirit of the old bones. Today we visited Cerro Quemado, the Burned Mountain—their sacred mountain—on a tourist excursion.

Just the two of us, the boy guide and I on small mountain horses, rode the roofs of the mountains, bare rock, stunted juniper, and pine. Nopal, sotol, lechuguilla, maguey, Joshua tree. On the summit a stone hut stored candles and artifacts. The guide invited me to go inside, but it was not his right to do so. Left on the rocks were coconut shell bowls with a coin pressed into the wax inside, bead designs of deer and humans fixed in wax, God's-eyes, prayer sticks, and pine incense. Fire circles. Everywhere on the mountain, I saw signs of prayer. Wixárika pilgrims entered Wirikuta; hunted the peyote with arrows, remembering the deer hunts of their former lands; and harvested them in baskets for the year ahead. Now in vans, stopping at sacred springs next to interstate highways, they transformed the modern world around them. From the western ocean where the sun dies to this mountain where the sun is born, this was the circuit of their world.

Pasadena, California, Spring 1963

My Caltech boyfriend Dennis the genius had just written to Sandoz for a bottle of mescaline, and they sent it. We measured out gel caps and ate ten each, having read *Drugs and the Mind* by

Robert S. de Ropp. We were on the beach in Venice, California, a run-down haunt of weight lifters and beatniks. They didn't notice us. Boundaries between us dissolved, and the van Gogh prints we had brought to look at invited us in. Warmth had taste, and social masks people wear became animal spirits. Colors invaded our sense receptors and bounced back at us amplified.

Dennis somehow drove us home after dark. Later, reading in my closet, I saw words burning on the page. I started to write poetry in my typing class. I was looking for a door.

Guadalajara, Jalisco, November 1995

I took a cab out to the Huichol museum, next to the church at Zapopan. The pressed bead designs woke up my color receptors and invited me back to another place and time. The cactus form was a friend; the other symbols were unknown to me, the meaning of the shaman, the deer, and the corn. The desert dwellers—scorpion, snake, and the datura flower of the Southwest—I knew. I bought the mask of the eclipse—the sun and moon crossing—the mask of the sun, the jaguar head, the scorpion, the drum, and the snake. I began to read about the people.

Santa Cruz, California, Spring 1978

The green peyote cacti arrived at Branciforte Drive in the spring, and we bought them. Rae Victor and I cut away the inner strychnine and ate the buttons blended with Rose's lime juice, the two bitter flavors competing enough that we could swallow. Green became a feeling, nauseating, almost rotten, the color of life, the blood of the plant world. Nine hours later we drank tequila to ground ourselves, the heavy breath of the redwood forest respiring its myriad jeweled light interactions. "The whole world is peyote," I said.

Zacatecas, November 1995

Zacatecas was built of rose stone into ochre sandstone cliffs, another mining town with a hell of seven circles named Eden. I flew here from Mexico City, watched by a narco with ostrich boots that matched his belt. He couldn't make me out and decided to let me be. Oddly, we shared a cab into town, he paying with rolls of bills stuffed in his jeans pocket. In the Zacatecan Museum I stumbled upon the 209 *bordados huicholes*, Huitchol embroideries, received by Francisco Benítez, a doctor who treated the Indians. They occupied the entire museum, and I took the journey of looking at all of them, the narratives of life invested with symbol, lived vividly, even as art. By the time I arrived at the depiction of the horse battle, the legs of the horses forming the border of the cloth, I was weeping. I don't know why I was so affected. Each picture had drawn me in, and I was no longer in Zacatecas, in a museum.

Later I visited the old Santa Ana mine. It had been dead for years and now was a disco reached by the miners' railroad. As I descended through the internal layers of the mine, I could see the ladders once used to carry ore to the surface, the ladders climbed by Indians with bags of rocks.

Wixárika were all about the town selling art, beaded necklaces, wax-pressed wooden sculptures, and embroidered bags. They were not far from their mountains in Nayarit, where their communities were still unreachable by outsiders. They narrowly escaped being the subjects of the Harvard Project, which found its home in San Cristóbal de las Casas, Chiapas—the founder, Evon Vogt, was afraid of the small, deadly scorpion that lived in the roof thatch in the sierra.

Later, working in the San Jose freight yard, I will see boxcar graffiti that says, "*Nalgas de Oro, Cañas, Zac.*" Butt cheeks of gold, Cañas, Zacatecas. Just down the road.

Real de Catorce, San Luis Potosí, April 2002

Back in Real de Catorce, there were many druggie people hanging around. They had that look. I was asked if I wanted peyote, but now I saw it as a rolling freight car, like alcohol, better left alone. For other reasons, too, better left alone so the Wixárika could continue to hunt it here, where their story placed it.

The boy guide who took me up Cerro Quemado and I were silent on the ride home, drifting. As we rode down off the mountain in the afternoon, the clouds were making shadows against the opposite canyon walls. Moving shadows, which, as we approached, became a herd of goats being driven home, in earth colors, gray and brown and white, moving as a second line under the clouds. A sand painting, a Two Grey Hills Navajo rug.

In the morning I went to the church of Saint Francis, the white facade and domed nave blinding against the scalloped ochre rock walls behind it. The sky was the color of the Virgin's blue robe. Black shadows painted architectural shapes as the sun traveled. Saint Francis had a room full of ex-votos, or painted tin pictures, thanking him. Lots of them involved rescue from trains. I could relate. Guadalupe had her chapel here, and in it were white doves against a rust tablecloth, an angel guardian in a blue robe, fresh flowers, and a golden tinsel streamer describing an arch. Lost in her presence, I heard my name.

"Hola, Linda," many feminine voices were calling me. The tourist police from San Luis were on an outing, like cream-colored Girl Scouts, in hats and pumps.

Leaving, I paused to look at Wixárika beads for sale on the street. "These always fly away," I said, handing a necklace back. I looked at a beaded bowl and pointed out the shaman in his feathered hat.

"You are the shaman," the Wixárika said, smiling.

Marietta, Georgia, Fall 2012

Ten years later, writing this story, it was October and the time for the Saint Francis pilgrimage. The news from Catorce was that nine members of the Zetas drug cartel were dead in a shootout with federal police. They had been staying in one of the Swiss hotels, extorting people and selling cocaine and pot. Pictures showed their seized armaments filling a room. I thought about the sinister vibe I'd felt around the druggie foreigners, and I had to admit that I had not stopped with peyote either.

The Wixárika were also in the news, since the government had licensed First Majestic Silver Corporation to mine again in the sacred desert. Their protest had drawn artists, sympathizers, and other indigenous groups to Catorce. Their presence probably also drew the Zetas. The Cerro Quemado was on YouTube, a magnet for New Age pilgrims. The Wixárika designated guardians to live in the desert and protect the peyote from non-Indians. Soldiers walked the streets of Catorce, arresting tourists for infractions.

"*Puro paracaidistas*," parachutists—squatters—a Mexican tourist wrote, "and filth in the streets. Not a magic town."

At home in Georgia, I looked at my Wixárika bag with a woven datura, their sacred and sinister tree of the wind; a plant I cultivated but had never used. It gives the ability to play the violin.

What did I see from the Cerro Quemado? I saw I had the desire to take peyote again, to change. I saw my past life, actions rippling in a pond. I saw rattlesnake sellers, my braking partner Al Stockton hunting rattlesnakes in the Union Pacific Alfalfa Yard in El Paso. I recalled reading the stories and studies of Wixárika religion, and I felt intrusive, seeing the ritual objects left in the sand, money in a jicara bowl, the wind blowing the prayer sticks. I remembered an acid peyote taste in my mouth, washed down with Rose's lime juice. I remembered the pure drug in gelatin caps from Sandoz that we took in Venice Beach, California. I imagined the train in the desert below, and I wondered where it crossed the border. Piedras Negras to Eagle Pass, Texas? I saw the migrant riders. I saw mystical seekers, drug takers, gangsters. I saw the mines from which the Wixárika fled the Spanish slave catchers; the land sliced by the train. I saw copper mines in El Paso and in Tucson, where I worked on the railroad, in the rattlesnake desert. Who was the observer? I was looking for a breath of home, the tracks of the itinerant railroad that created my current homelessness, in spite of digging into the red clay soil of where I lived now.

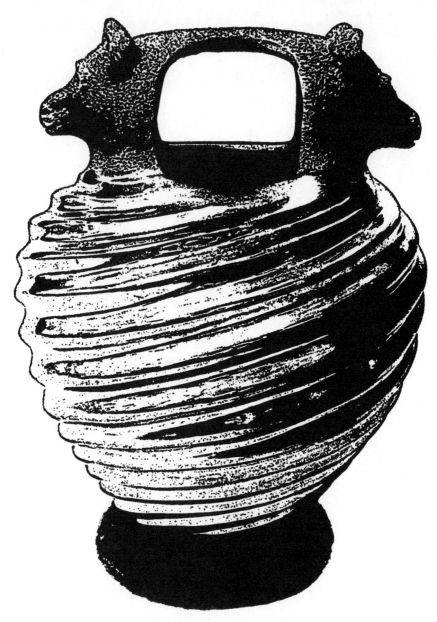

Héctor Ortega, Bear Head Pot, Casas Grandes, Chihuahua, 2004. Clay, 8 ×
6.5 in. Private collection.

The Cave of the Olla

Mata Ortiz, Chihuahua, February 2004

THE POT IN a Mexico City crafts store called to me. A glass-burnished spiral with two bear heads for a handle, coil built in the old way, wood fired, black, and fragile. Four hundred US dollars. I touched it, the rough volcanic fur, the smooth seashell body. I put it back. Héctor Ortega, Mata Ortiz, a pottery village in Chihuahua. I would go there sometime.

Spring break 2004 at Kennesaw State University in Georgia. It was my fourth year teaching, and I wanted a taste of the West. My companion was a potter, so I would take her there, I thought. Travelocity, credit card, round trip to Tucson, stay with friend Leslie, shuttle to the border at Agua Prieta, bus from there. As I was a former train conductor, trips were my thing. Point A to point B. I could set things in motion. I had worked on the border for years, running freight trains out of El Paso and Tucson. Day turned into night in the dreamtime of riding trains with the mirage landscape streaming past the open window. A river of memories now, locked into scent and images.

We set out, Caroline and I, both short haired, middle aged, wearing jeans and sneakers, no makeup, carry-on bags only.

Caroline came from the Georgia Mountains. We both spoke Spanish. She had studied art in San Miguel de Allende years ago, ridden horseback in her husband's tuxedo when he cheated on her there, but had not been a traveler for years. I was the conductor. Leslie picked us up at the airport and drove us into the west side hills. Caroline had never been to the desert. She was looking around.

"Is this place landscaped?" she said.

I could see what she meant. In Georgia, a place of deciduous trees, every year the leaves are gathered up and hauled away, and pine straw, bought from a big-box home store, is scattered in their place. The desert, of course, landscapes itself.

Later, on a walk, Caroline photographed Leslie. She had one of the first digital cameras and was learning to use it. She was never afraid of technology and trusted her hands to teach her. The world went through her artist's lens and came out remade.

"Good luck getting that to come out," I said. I had tried to photograph Leslie for years, and none of the images had ever materialized. Finally, she had sent me pictures of herself. I knew it was one of Leslie's magical aspects, of which there were many.

In the morning we left for the border. The shuttle ran out of a shopping mall in South Tucson down to Douglas. I had worked in the Phelps Dodge plant there, switching out ore cars in the 1970s. I still remembered the highline track, the black silt that worked its way through boots to stain your socks, and the rivers of fiery ore that lit up the night. The highway angled across the bottom of the state where Sonora, Mexico, joins Chihuahua—the Chiricahua Mountains always a conduit for Apaches and other travelers. Brown hills rose like old friends, creating for me a feeling of nostalgic peace. It was odd how safe I felt working on trains, odd because the work was so dangerous. The company that harried us also protected us—a paradox of the whole West. Alone you were coyote bait, but under the wing of a ranch, mine, railroad, or military base, you were part of something greater than yourself. Even the scalp hunters roamed in bands. Leaving the railroad, I still carried that feeling of safety with me down into Mexico, wherever I went.

Today we went on foot after the shuttle left us in Douglas. Wheeling our luggage over the bridge into Agua Prieta, we picked up tourist cards and asked about a hotel. I never traveled at night in Mexico, and it was too late in the day to reach Nuevo Casas Grandes, the setting-out point for Mata Ortiz.

"Hacienda Motel," we were told. "The best hotel in Agua Prieta."

Checking in, I noticed something odd. The parking spaces facing the entrance were taped off, and Chevy Blazers with fit young men in the drivers' seats were parked next to them. "Bodyguards," I thought. The manager didn't seem surprised that we were on foot, and we wheeled our luggage to our upstairs room, which faced the interior courtyard. Eyes followed us. I remembered another motel room, in the city center of Houston, when I was working there during the oil boom. At night, drunks would call the room or bang on the door. I would just wait it out, but I wished for a pistol, in case they tried to come in.

Today, though, the sun was shining, and Agua Prieta was ours.

"Let's go and look at cowboy boots," I said.

When I worked in Douglas on the railroad, there were rumors of boots over the border. The rumors were true. Along with stores selling Mennonite cheese, many western stores lined the dusty streets, with pastel full-quill ostrich boots and matching belts in the storefront windows. Prices started at $300. "Who's buying these?" I thought. Such boots and pristine

Stetson straw hats were narco uniforms. It was not easy for a woman to enter these stores, since the boots were all for men. At last we found a corner store, Bob's Boots, with a cluttered, dusty look. Shoeboxes were piled high. We went in and were left alone. I walked out with a pair of men's peacock-blue zippered ankle boots in smooth ostrich, Mexican size 5.5, with two-inch heels. Another successful transgression.

Back at the motel, things were going on. As we came out of the restaurant, a cab arrived, and a uniformed officer emerged and went upstairs to what I now could see to be a conference room, directly across from the taped parking spaces. A ripple went through the bodyguards, like night ducks on a pond. I could imagine them saying, "The two women, old and short haired, no makeup, who are they?"

"Nuns," I thought. "They think we are nuns." I was glad I didn't wear the ostrich cowboy boots back from the store. Caroline and I went up to our room and settled in for the night. After midnight, somebody knocked on the door, but we didn't answer, and the night guest passed on. In the morning, we wheeled out early, conscious of the clatter we made on the concrete walkways. We took a cab to the bus station and booked seats to Nuevo Casas Grandes, the early spring solanos blowing "Texas rain" through the wire fences that fronted the highway.

We passed through Janos, home of the cheese, and turned south, paralleling the Sierra Madre. Casas Grandes, or Paquimé, was an ancient city on the north-south trade route. Leslie had told me that a meteorite was found there and the people had buried it as if it were a person. They also raised scarlet macaws, which Leslie said were used instead of humans in sacrifice. The people of Casas Grandes were famous potters who created designs that gave rise to the revival started in Mata Ortiz by Juan Quezada, who, I was happy to learn, was a former railroad worker. The railroad town for me, the pots for Caroline. Guidebooks on Paquimé kept referring to a Cueva de la Olla, Cave of the Pot, a large ceramic granary in a cliff dwelling nearby, but Nuevo Casas Grandes was not a typical tourist location. Nobody had heard of the cave, or if they had, they described it as "far away," and no, there was no transportation there. Looking back, I can see that I really had no idea about the geography of where we were.

Finally, Caroline and I hired a taxi driver to take us the twenty miles to Mata Ortiz, a fare he regretted once his taxi hit the wash that was the road. The valley, though, was rural Mexico, and every mode of transportation was on the move, burro cart, bicycle, horse, pickup, and feet. We passed Colonia Juárez, one Mormon town among many in Mexico. At last the road branched around a cottonwood tree, and we entered a prosperous adobe town with tasteful restaurants and B and Bs. It couldn't have felt more different from the tumbleweed towns we had passed through since crossing the border. The reason was employment. Everyone was throwing pots, pots that sold for thousands in the Southwest art mart. Now the guidebook was accurate, and we settled in at Jorge Quintana's. Jorge looked vaguely Chinese, and he told us how his grandfather, a Chinese cook, had escaped being shot by Pancho Villa's raiders.

"Pancho Villa hated Chinese," he said, "and when his men raided, Grandfather hid under the table in the kitchen. He had just cooked a big pot of chow mein, and Villa's men liked it, so when they found him they told him he could live if he kept cooking."

Jorge set Caroline up to make pots with his neighbors, Ismael Flores and his wife, María Loya. María hand built the pots on her kitchen table, and soon she and Caroline were working beside each other as if they had been doing it for years. Ismael applied the designs once the pots were dry, and then they wood fired them in their yard. Traditional wood-fired pots were wanted by the buyers, but it represented potentially wasted days for the potters, who risked losing their work at the caprice of the fire.

"Was there anything you wanted to do while you were here?" they asked.

"Well," we said, "we want to go to the Cave of the Olla, but nobody knows how to get there."

"We know," they said. "How about tomorrow morning?"

Preparations involved sending their two daughters with us to the store to buy provisions. We would get the gas and the lunch. They would pick us up at dawn.

"*Chorizos, cebollas, ajo, tomates, papas, tortillas, arroz, chiles, manteca, galletas, refrescos, cerveza, carne, cerillos, café, tomatillos, vinagre.*" The children kept pointing at more food items as the bags filled up. There were six of us, no? Seventy-four dollars later, we left the store, wondering.

No matter, tomorrow was the cave. Back in our room, people with pots were beginning to knock on the door. Each room had a display area, two barrels with a plank between them. Ours was soon covered with pots, as was the bed. I had wanted to buy seed pots, miniature granaries with a small hole for the seeds to enter. I was a datura cultivator and collected the seeds for next year's planting, but how to store them? I was using an old pepper jar until a houseguest almost shook them on her eggs one morning. Datura was the sorcerer's plant, tree of the wind, jimsonweed, ingredient in zombification formulas. I needed a suitable container. I needed a seed pot. Meanwhile, Caroline was changing out her digital camera's cards. The one with Leslie's picture on it would later disappear. No surprise.

The potters showed up at dawn in a Bronco, and the six of us headed west across the desert toward the blue mountains. After an hour we started to climb, still on a dirt road, up switchbacks whose curves revealed hulks of cars nose down in the arroyos below.

"*Muchos accidentes,*" María told us. "*Borrachos.*" Many drunken accidents. I was never far from a 12 Step reminder. I could always see myself in a parallel life having gone off the edge.

We were still in a desert environment, but when we finally crested the mountain, the road curved down into another niche, a protected valley with fruit orchards, pastures, and farmhouses. One of these was our destination, a white clapboard ranch house in a peach orchard. Cajón de sorpresas. María's parents and her grandmother, holding a small baby, came out on the porch to greet us. We ate breakfast. Afterward, in the Bronco, we were now ten, including the baby. Off to the Cave of the Olla, winding down dirt roads for another hour.

We emerged into a sandy wash on a canyon floor. It's odd how cliff dwellings all feel the same. Protected, as peaceful as a grave, existing in human, not geological, time. We were on the Continental Divide, where a chain of cliff dwellings, more ancient than those of the Southwest Pueblo Indians, also ran north–south. In this range to the south, modern cliff dwellers, the Rarámuris, still lived in the old way, their stronghold protected by 6,000-foot canyons. I was surprised that there was no guard. Cows wandered freely, and a shallow river made snake curves under cottonwoods. We parked the Bronco and started unloading. Ismael pointed out the way to the cave, up a little trail.

The *olla* dominated the cave, which also contained apartments; it was fifteen feet high, a perfect adobe pot. I took Caroline's hand, and we stood there looking at it. One of the reasons we got along was that she didn't say a lot, and I could be left with my own thoughts. I assumed we shared them, as we now shared this space. "Not a bad gift for a potter," I thought.

The sides of the canyon cut by the river were home to many other cliff dwellings, all of them in the same unprotected state as this cave. It was like going back in time 150 years, when the northern versions of these homes were first "discovered" by Anglos. I thought, "Well, the government obviously has other fish to fry here," the obvious one being the drug war, though there was no sign of its presence at the moment.

Back at the car, the purpose of the shopping trip was becoming clear. Ismael had pulled out a folding cast-iron grill, and a family feast was in progress. The fragrance of blistered chorizo, chiles, and garlic carried on the air. The women were warming tortillas and passing them out with the grilled meat. Caroline and I settled down under a tree, leaned back, and shared the meal.

"I am now as far away as it is possible to be from Georgia," I thought, looking around. It was a hammock of time, carrying more than its share.

We adults all rested there in the shade while the children played among the ruins. When the sun slanted from the west, we packed up the car and retraced our route. At the farmhouse the grandparents sent us on our way with preserved peaches and picked chiles, replenishing the gift. We started to climb back over the Continental Divide. Now logging trucks were on the road with us, dwarfing the Bronco, which sputtered and struggled and finally stopped. A fine blanket of dust covered all of us inside the car, Ismael and five women. He got out and popped the hood. Soon the driver of the blocked logging truck behind us joined him. After an hour, as we were losing the light, we all pushed the Bronco to the side of the road, and the logging truck passed us and stopped. The driver got out and attached a chain from the back of the truck to the Bronco. We all got in. Up we went over the divide, staring at hundreds of tree rings. I tried not to think about what I knew about shifting loads. *Como México, no hay dos.* There are not two like Mexico.

Over the crest, we unhooked, and the Bronco sputtered to life on the downgrade. We would sleep tonight in our beds, the blue desert blanket before us. We blinked awake just before Mata Ortiz, the ghost tree sentinel appeared in the road, and we knew we were back. We went into our room, arms full of presents out of the supposedly narco-infested sierra.

Héctor Ortega, the bear-head potter, didn't live in Mata Ortiz. Asking around, we got an address in Nuevo Casas Grandes and turned up unannounced the next day. Héctor was firing pots in his backyard. Yes, he had a bear-head pot for sale. And so when we took our seats on the bus for the border, I was holding in my lap, wrapped like a baby, his fragile spiral black pot, burnished with an obsidian stone. It was morning, and we would reach Tucson by nightfall. All was well. We had treasures, gifts, and knowledge. I looked out the window, as I had done riding trains on the other side, and saw the same brown mountains marking the horizon. I realized that I had wanted a return. I had gotten sober in El Paso and worked out a new path for my life, riding trains across this landscape. It was for me the terrain of redemption, unexpected, painful, and woundingly beautiful. Riding trains in the summer, I had seen the migrants lying under the cars on sidings to get out of the sun. They all looked like teenagers. Because of them, I started to learn Spanish, which had allowed me to travel to the other side.

The migrants were with us now, on the bus. Their dreams of redemption were different from mine, their border not so easily crossable. This was not the same bus we rode down on. People were dressed from the southern part of Mexico. No one was talking loudly, and their eyes were on the floor. At checkpoints, soldiers got on and walked the aisles, looking and asking questions. Several young men were taken off, and the bus resumed its journey. The haze of the border we were headed toward was now a cold passing hand.

I held Héctor's pot in my arms, feeling the fragility of its shell. The meteorite child buried as a human. Migrant dreams. Travelers for art or desire. Borders, armies, governments, men with guns. Caroline and I had easy passage, with our white cracka asses, mistaken for nuns.

Huipil, San Andrés Larráinzar, Chiapas, 1993. Backstrap-loomed wool, 38 × 42 in. Private collection.

The Strength of the Maya Woman

Chiapas, Summer 2004

I REMEMBER THE first time I saw a play by the Maya women's theater group Fortaleza de la Mujer Maya, or FOMMA. It was in the early 1990s, and I was visiting Chiapas. The play seemed simplistic to me and the female actors, untrained. Marcey and Janet, in their role of leftist feminist critics upholding artistic standards, panned them. Looking back, I see I had no way to begin to understand what I had witnessed.

To start with, the fact that they were performing at all was revolutionary. Maya women did not take performance roles in public. They had also written the play. Maya women did not read and write or often even speak Spanish, the language the play was in. The play was about having to marry a drunk who beat you, in order to stay alive. The subject was taboo and had gotten the women thrown out of a different, official Maya theater group. And the performance was held outside the old church, where other Maya women, most of them refugees from the surrounding traditional communities, sold textiles and lived desperate lives. Now this group was speaking for them.

Mimi Laughlin, the wife of Robert, the anthropologist who

sponsored the official House of the Writer theater group, had taken this group under her wing. "It almost caused a divorce," she told me later. Marcey and Janet's critique, then, was directed to Mimi, who had persuaded them to attend. San Cristóbal de las Casas had its circles, which resulted from the melding of the expat artists' colony with the Harvard Chiapas Project anthropologists and the invitation into the conversation of indigenous artists that both groups attracted. Within the hierarchy of gatekeepers, this group of Maya women belonged outside, except that Mimi had gotten them funded and housed through her informal connections.

"Not at the level we expected," was Janet's assessment. Marcey and Janet made sharp distinctions. It was what kept them alive and interested for so long.

Ten years later, in 2004, after we had become friends, Mimi asked me to do something for FOMMA.

"Why don't you come and give us a writing workshop?" she said.

"Sure," I responded, thinking how impossible it would be for me. In the first place, how would I do it in Spanish? Well, I would have the handbook that I used for my writing classes, and Mimi could translate it for me, if necessary. As it turned out, friends, with me in Oaxaca the month before, made off with my book, so I was on my own with only what I remembered. I planned to come for two weeks, thinking the women would want a few days. I had already experienced being asked to share what I knew in Oaxaca, in the days when I could hardly speak at all. In Mexico you were a part of the collective, whether you realized it or not. It was the way they did things. So I took a notebook and outlined what I normally taught in sixteen weeks into a few pages. It also dawned on me that the women in FOMMA weren't native Spanish speakers either. That made me feel better. We would muddle through.

FOMMA's house in Barrio de Mexicanos, financed originally by Mimi and Bob, was undergoing renovations. They were getting a grant to create a covered theater space, an alternative to the open courtyard where they now performed. Upstairs, a sewing factory was busy, and downstairs were literacy classrooms and an Internet café. Kees Grootenboer, the Mexican architect whose work was all over town, was undertaking the project. FOMMA was doing OK.

I met the founders first, Petrona de la Cruz Cruz and Isabel Juárez Espinoza, whose offices faced each other across the courtyard. We were going to do an exchange. They would grant me interviews and a theater performance. I would give them this workshop. After the interviews, the other members assembled— Victoria, Francisca, Margarita, Emma, Marta, Petrona's son José, and Mimi. We pulled wooden chairs up around a table and made our introductions. I then laid out the creative nonfiction writing spectrum, from *diario personal*, memoir, to *cuentos sobre viajes*, travel stories, to *arte del performance*, performance art, to *testimonio*, testimony, to *periodismo*, journalism. Because they made theater out of the stories of their daily lives, this kind of writing suited them. We went over the conventions and all did a writing exercise, imagining an ideal reader and a worst critic. We then went around the circle reading our work aloud.

We had now spent three hours together, and I decided to wrap up. I gave them homework: to write a true story about their lives.

"When do you want to meet again?" I asked them, thinking in a few days.

"Tomorrow," they said unanimously. This went on for a week. The next day we went around the table reading. Everyone had produced something. Victoria didn't speak Spanish yet, so when it was her turn, she stood up and told a story in Tzotzíl, her native Maya language. Victoria was a shepherdess, and her story was about a shepherdess caring for the sheep and singing to the trees. A big storm came up, and she herded the sheep into a cave they used for shelter in the winter. It got dark. Something about the storm—the immense lightning, the sound of trees breaking—frightened her more than usual. She thought of her husband, who did not know where she was. She decided to leave the sheep and go home. That night, she had a bad dream about lost sheep in which her mother told her the sheep went to sleep in a cloud. Her husband was looking for them; she was looking for them. In the dream, she was told to take fire back to the cave. After the storm, she and her husband went to find the sheep. A coyote had found them in the cave, and only one sheep escaped. Her husband cried.

When I asked what the story was about, Victoria said, "Choice."

All of the women in FOMMA had sacrificed to be part of the collective. They had chosen to stay in the cave with the sheep and not return to their husbands or traditional life. Francisca wrote about having to get on an airplane for the first time to go to Mexico City, where she would get her visa to go to the United States for a performance. She was waiting to board, frightened out of her mind, but she told herself, "I need to do this for FOMMA," and that gave her the courage to get on the plane. Mimi told me later that Francisca's husband had beaten her so badly when she told him she was going to travel that her face was almost unrecognizable. He also threatened to lock her out of the house when she returned and to never allow her to see her children. In spite of this, she flew, and when she returned she divorced him and got custody of the children.

The group was going to come to the United States again, near where I lived, and I decided to bring them to my school, Kennesaw State University, as an add-on. The first week of school, normally a crush of boring administrative hot air, I started glad-handing for their visit. I hit up deans and department chairs for money. To my surprise, no one said no. The usually unavailable Stillwell Theater was available. They wouldn't have to stay on the floor of my home—there was money for a hotel, our usually penny-pinching comptroller told me, two suites, in fact. There was money for a van to drive them around. Remembering what Mimi's husband had told me about bringing the original theater group to the States and how hungry they were all the time, I went to Costco beforehand and stocked their hotel rooms with snack packs, popcorn, Snickers, crackers, and Coca-Cola.

When they arrived they came into the rooms, grabbed Snickers bars and popcorn, and started bouncing on the beds like teenagers. The first night we had dinner at my house, which has been described as "a Mexican installation." We had tamales from a hair salon that sold them for a local cook. The Maya women all ritually washed their hands before touching the food. They looked at every object in the house that came from Mexico, the textiles from Chiapas in particular, and the dance masks, and a photograph of small boys playing Jesus on some crosses in front of a church, taken by the San Cristóbal photographer Gayle Walker. They discussed this picture, asking me if it was a joke. "Yes," I said. They liked that. They also liked it that I had a machete hanging on the door. Their energy warmed up the house, and I loved sharing it with them.

The next morning, they came over for scrambled eggs and tortillas. After breakfast, I was about to dump the leftover scrambled eggs into the garbage when someone rushed over to stop me. I got the point. When I asked them what they wanted to see, they all said, "The Dollar Store." Returning migrants had mentioned that store, and they had orders from home. So we went there, and they bought children's clothes, T-shirts, and tablecloths. But first we needed to go to an ATM. Isabel inserted her card, but nothing happened. Petrona looked at the camera eye and said, "They can tell we are Mexicans. That's why it won't come out."

When they visited my classes, the usual dynamic changed. They asked the students to tell them what they did as work and how they could afford to go to school. The students then became pizza delivery persons, waiters, retail clerks, babysitters, cooks, parking lot attendants, and IT repair persons. The students started asking what FOMMA did and found shepherds, weavers, maids, homemakers, salespeople, tailors, and gardeners.

"What does it look like to you here?" the students asked.

"The houses are closed up tight, and people don't walk outside. You don't even see animals, not even a dog on the streets, not even garbage, not even dirt. Everyone is alone in their cars," Victoria said.

There was a large Maya immigrant community up the road in Canton, centered around the Our Lady of La Salette Catholic Church. The FOMMA women donated a performance to them. That Sunday, the large community room filled up with Maya, mostly men. The Maya women who attended the church were also invited, but many stayed home to prepare the lunch that would follow. The men were expecting folkloric dancing. Instead, these demure women in Maya dress disappeared behind the improvised curtain and reappeared as men drinking in a bar. The men in the audience exchanged glances. This was not going to be a ballet; this play was about them. But the FOMMA women were funny. They knew exactly how drunken men acted. They were credible.

The play, *I Grew Up with My Mother's Love*, portrayed the husband's bad treatment of his wife and daughter, due to his choosing to drink instead of accepting his life as a farmer. The mother carried the burden of raising the daughter and grounding her in Maya culture. The poetry of the culture flowed through the blessings of the midwife's character:

Welcome to this house, to the blessed earth, in her will you
　pass
Your youth, until you become a woman.

Your heart will be a warrior, curious and strong like the
　nagual of your birth.
You will fly, enjoying everything that surrounds you. Lovely
　butterfly.

The play resolved through a dream in which the husband saw himself killing his wife. He changed his ways. Dreams, portals to the supernatural, are more real than this earthly life.

"His reformation wasn't believable," Mimi said, "given all that came before. But then, this is the way they want it. They're tired of unhappy endings. Now they have a chance to write the plot and make it come out right."

Following the play, we all shared a meal cooked by the Canton Maya women. After the meal, the men discretely disappeared, and the women gathered together to discuss larger issues. In this group were women who had been forced to abandon their children in order to emigrate. The play FOMMA would perform at

Kennesaw the next day was about such an abandoned family. Some members had relevant personal memories. Isabel had been sent to San Cristóbal at the age of eight to work as a maid, and Petrona had been expelled from her house and community when her mother died. Many points of view were speaking here. I felt honored to hear them. I doubted there were many places where this dialogue could happen.

Then there was the matter of traditional clothing. "Why do you abandon the *traje*, the traditional dress?" Isabel asked. In Chiapas, the women maintain the clothing traditions, since the men often work abroad or in mestizo plantations and adopt Western dress.

I knew that Maya clothing was valued in the Canton community, since the local Guatemalan grocery store sold lengths of cloth and huipils from Huehuetenango.

"It is expensive, and it calls attention," one of the local Maya answered.

"That is a sadness," Isabel said.

The subject turned to alcohol and family violence. Francisca, who had played the role of the abusive drunken husband, testified that in fourteen years of marriage she had been repeatedly beaten by her husband. FOMMA had shown her that she did not have to remain silent and that through acting she had a way to transform the experience and to help others.

"I implore you," she said, "to speak up."

The women in the room were listening intently.

"How do you begin?" someone asked.

"Little by little, and then you continue," Francisca answered.

At Kennesaw State University, the women played to a full house, and at the end we showered them with Costco roses. Afterward, even though it was late, the women were hungry. I was thinking late-night snack, but at the Marietta Diner, they ordered full plates of fried shrimp and French fries, topped off by banana splits. They boxed every leftover, and with the dozen roses apiece, they got on the plane to return home the next day.

Now my penance began, as I received a personal request from the dean that, in return for her $500, I serve on a tenure and promotion guidelines committee that met every Friday for three hours for the next six months.

"You sacrificed for FOMMA," Isabel said with a smile when I told her about it.

Casa Felicitas Workshop, Coyote Head Pot, Santa Clara del Cobre, Michoacán, 1995. Copper, 18 × 12 in. Private collection.

Farewell

Cuenca, Ecuador, Summer 2009

TWO WEEKS BEFORE I and a group of students were leaving for Chiapas, the US State Department issued a travel warning for all of Mexico because of the swine flu. No matter that Georgia had more cases than Chiapas at the time. I called a meeting and told the students, "We are turning left. We are going to Ecuador." And we did.

This meant I was traveling south but not going to see Marcey for the first time in eighteen years. When I had visited her the summer before, she had just recovered her cat, Luli, from a kidnapping episode. A reclusive black Persian, Luli had disappeared, and after months, Marcey's friends had found another black Persian and introduced her as Luli to Marcey, who took her in without saying much. Apparently this new Luli would sleep on the bed, something the old Luli had disdained, so her suspicions were aroused. I called Marcey shortly afterward.

"I have decided to use the *agua purificada* truck to call Luli," Marcey told me. "What do you think of it?"

I thought about her riding the truck, dragging its chain through the streets, calling her cat over their loudspeaker, and it made me sad.

"Maybe not a great idea," I said.

"We'll see," Marcey said.

A week later, she had her cat back, the other Luli returned to sender.

"How can you doubt me?" Marcey said.

Every year, when I said good-bye to her, Marcey would tell me, "Don't think I am going to be here forever."

"My Jewish mother," I thought, but it did keep me coming back, in a kind of magic ritual. "First year I'm going to miss," I thought, superstitiously.

The summer study in Ecuador went smoothly, Kennesaw having connections there through the Education Department's teacher exchange program. We stayed in Quito and explored the Avenue of the Volcanoes, dropping down on either side to cloud forests and jungle hot springs. My hotel was right across the street from a dance studio run by Sylvia García, a passionate tango dancer, and every day I danced tango with her for an hour under the volcanoes. I then went back to my hotel and slept for eighteen hours. Quito was at 9,350 feet.

After the students returned home, my friend Margo, of Guadalajara fame, joined me, and we traveled south by bus. In Baños, we caught a wild ride with a German hotel owner, who took us to Cuenca, driving 80 mph, often on two wheels. I loved it. Margo hated it. Cuenca was in a different eco-niche than Quito, much lower and easier to live in. We went up to Bullcay, where weavers used imported silk thread to weave ikat shawls on backstrap looms. Margo was being frugal. I was not. When we returned to Cuenca, after our excursion, I went to an Internet café and found I had an e-mail from Carter, my friend who had introduced me to

Marcey all those years ago. She had died the night before—just laid down and died, a month short of ninety-eight.

Out in the square, the students of the Universidad Católica de Cuenca were celebrating the day. They had brought piles of fireworks, rockets, and a *castillo*, a bamboo castle to hold fireworks that are fired off at intervals, culminating in a spectacular finale. As it got dark, they set the rockets off endlessly, the park becoming a site of explosion and descending ash. I found a bench and let the street celebration take me. They were working their way up to the castillo, which they set afire after about four hours of warm-up. What really got me, though, were the lanterns that followed until midnight, colored paper quadrangles mounted on wooden crosses that held wicks so that the lanterns lofted up above the tile roofs, silent and beautiful, after the rockets, like messengers.

Vicente Hernández Vásquez, *Devil on Cross*, San Martín Tilcajete, Oaxaca, 2006. Wood, 20 × 13 × 3.75 in. Private collection.

CHAPTER FOURTEEN

The Fun Train to Chiapas

Chiapas, June 2010

NOT SINCE MY days as a conductor on the Fun Train to Reno, penitence for all the times I spent carousing in other people's workplaces, had I been so unwillingly connected to a passel of drunks. Our study abroad group was going to San Cristóbal this year because of the continuing teachers' strike in Oaxaca. I had an assistant, Lupita, and eighteen students—or "bunnies," as I came to think of them in an attempt to reframe their constant cognitive shortcomings, as in, "Bunnies lose their credit cards because bunnies don't have pockets."

"Well, down the hatch," Lola, the former stewardess, said, slamming tequila at Rosa's Deli for lunch during our layover in Houston. An odd way to prepare to fly to an airport in a hot country, where a bus would meet us for the hour-long drive to a colonial town at 7,000 feet, at which point the family she would be staying with for a month would meet her for the first time.

"*Science News*, anyone?" I asked the long row of bored-looking students waiting for the connecting flight. No takers. Eventually some students plugged in their cell phones and iPods to charge and then set off for other parts of the airport, leaving their expensive devices behind. I had mentioned that in Mexico three dollars a day is an average wage.

I settled in to catching up on breaking news in microbiology. After an hour, our connecting flight to Tuxtla was called, and we started boarding. Five students were missing. I alerted the gate workers, since the flight was oversold and a honeymoon couple was pleading for seats.

"We're a group," I said. "And people are meeting us in Tuxtla."

Just then a trolley meant for handicapped passengers arrived, with three of my students aboard.

"We were shopping," they said. "In another terminal."

Two students missing. I boarded the plane. They had all signed an agreement that if they became separated from the group, they had to meet us at our next destination at their own expense. Oh, those university lawyers, always thinking ahead.

As the flight crew was preparing for takeoff, the remaining students ran up the gangplank, wheezing. Everybody in the hutch—for now.

When we disembarked in Tuxtla, a row of folkloric dancers was waiting with plumeria leis and a marimba band. Flashbulbs went off, and a reporter corralled Kevin, the student who was the first person off the plane, for an interview. Our flight, it turned out, was the first direct Houston-to-Tuxtla service, and we got the red carpet treatment. I hoped Kevin's parents weren't watching TV, but then the news blackout in the United States about Mexico was probably on my side. His parents had already tried to bribe him with the price of the trip if he would just stay home. They were middle class and convinced he was going to be kidnapped and held for ransom if he set foot in Mexico. I met with him before the trip in a coffeehouse in Marietta to try to calm him down.

"I want to be an anthropologist," he said.

"Well, you know," I said, "Chiapas was the site of the Harvard Project, and even now, if you throw a stone, you hit an anthropologist. They used to hand out water purification pills and send the students out to live with shamans. Our arrangements are posh by comparison."

It was the rainy season, which usually meant downpours lasting twenty minutes in the afternoons and occasionally all night. But our first field trip, a ride in an open boat through the 3,000-foot Sumidero Canyon, was scheduled for the morning, and I thought the drizzle would clear up further down the mountain. Besides, I had told the students to bring rain gear. So what if we got a little wet? It would be a warm rain. I had paid in advance through the school, a wonderful convenience if all went according to plan, but when we arrived at the launches, the rain angled into cold needles against our skin. The boats were running, however, since Mexican operations, particularly those that have already been paid for, run no matter what. It reminded me of working on the railroad, which operated around the clock in any weather.

"OK," I said. "Get your rain gear on, and those sunglasses and a hat will really be useful."

A good percentage of the students were in flip-flops and navel-baring T-shirts. One had no rain gear at all. Another student was shivering and confided to me she could not swim.

"Sit next to me," I said. "I'll pull you out."

We set off, a bark of fools. If you pulled the hood of your raincoat up, put your hat and sunglasses on, and made a breathing hole, you could keep your face to the wind and see ahead. The boats were speedboats, and the crew loved to go fast. Above us the canyon grew taller as waterfalls and orchids spilled down the walls. The students were taking selfies on their cell phones. They were starting to have fun.

Instead of the rain letting up, as it usually did, it got heavier as the trip went on. We stopped for lunch at the dam, and the students pretty much stuck to the one-beer-while-a-trip-is-in-progress rule I had imposed after experiences with a similar group of drunks in Ecuador.

"You never know," I said, "what is going to happen on a field trip." It was a cultural thing, the "if God wills it" part of every declaration of intention made in Mexico, where serendipity is an art form.

Since we were all waterlogged and the rain was now inundating the highway, fogging the windows, and running down the aisle of the bus, we were taking back to town and I called off the side trip to Chiapa de Corzo in the afternoon. It was dawning on me that we were experiencing an unusual weather event. It was Hurricane Alex, which would traverse Chiapas, pour rain for three days, pick up power over the Gulf, and destroy large parts of Monterrey in the week that followed. We all had to buy knee-high rubber boots to walk around town.

San Cristóbal de las Casas, the old colonial capital of the state of Chiapas, was Maya in culture and feudal in history. The town was the daily commerce center for the surrounding indigenous villages and the seat of the famous bishop, Bartolomé de las Casas, who argued the case in 1540 that the Indians had souls. It was a magnet for Harvard anthropologists, black-sheep Mexican artists, and wandering hippies. It was notorious for drunks. Firecrackers exploded all night in the foggy alleys. In 1994 the town performed revolution as the Zapatistas made a symbolic raid on the city archives. Since the new road from Tuxtla was built, however, the town had transformed itself into a happening night spot. Two *andadores*, pedestrian streets, transected the center of town and were lined with bars and restaurants. People would drive up from Tuxtla and roll back down the highway in the wee hours. I remembered the Maya boys I used to see sledding firewood on the old mountain road, steering among trucks, buses, and cars.

Some students, meanwhile, were happily sledding from bar to bar on what locals termed the true "Ruta Maya." Walking into the Argentine restaurant one night, I got the cold shoulder. It seemed the students had been ordering drinks and not paying the tab. When I walked down the street, I pretended not to see them lying on café floors, having fallen out of their chairs. The group was splitting into party timers and serious participants, who were giving me frequent updates on the former's bad behavior.

"Look," I said, "don't turn up hung over for our field trips, since we will be three hours on mountain roads in a bus. No turnouts." This was before I had discovered biodegradable barf bags.

Unfortunately we missed checking Lola, the former stewardess, before she got on the bus. About an hour into the trip to the Toniná ruins, Lupita pointed out that she was lying down on a seat, pale and nauseated. Other students told me that she had been out drinking the night before. When we arrived at the site, she could hardly walk and clearly couldn't hike in the heat. While everyone else went with the guide, I stayed behind with Lola in an accommodating restaurant, where they were extraordinarily polite in spite of the fact that she was lying down on their concrete floor and making frequent exits to throw up in their bushes. I just kept buying Sprites, and the young woman behind the counter kept smiling.

"Mexico is so forgiving," I thought. I was also wondering where the nearest I.V. was likely to be in case Lola went into shock. Of course, I took the opportunity to 12 Step her. That's the 12-Step program slang for telling her how it had been for me, what had happened, and what it was like now. After all, she was a captive audience. I had been like these students for nearly half my adult life. Only I had never made it out of the country as a drunk. I couldn't get up the road to Berkeley from my mountain cabin in Santa Cruz. It had taken the Southern Pacific Railroad to break me of my habits and sober me up. Sink or swim. Remembering how close to sinking I had come, I worried for the students. Was I their keeper? My plans for the month were more in the line of getting in some writing time. I would have one glass of water with them, avoiding the bar tab, and then split. I didn't want to see their Facebook pages or their cell phone photos of the night before.

"Walk of shame," Lola said as I helped her into the bus for the return trip. I knew she wasn't done yet.

Of the drinkers, Brittany was the ringleader, the one who came out of the toilet smelling like a rose. "Oh my God," she said, "You see that guy in the checked pants? I think I fucked him last night."

"That's all you have?" I said. "Checked pants?"

I have to say I have been there, done that. Madame Bovary, she is I: 1966 Los Angeles Summer of Love and lots of other summers of love. But before AIDS, before mutation. Sex doesn't care. Giardia doesn't care.

I ran into Ronald, one of the students, on the andador. We had to stop and discuss Kierkegaard. Ronald was well read and smart but religion bound. He was determined to reconcile philosophy with his archaic Christian beliefs. "Good luck," I thought, but at least you could talk to him for more than five minutes without tearing your hair out. He saw me trying to send a message on my cell phone.

"Here," he said, taking it and demonstrating a texting strategy.

"You have to scroll through the letter options on this model. Tiresome, but possible."

"Thanks," I said. "Let me buy you a sherbet. Is repetition possible?"

Ronald was always trying to figure out Spanish idioms from dictionaries. Like most techies, for him personal interaction was a last resort.

"You have to get idioms from conversation," I said. "That means you have to talk to actual people, like your homestay family." Ronald had a tendency to let his iPad do his interacting for him. When Lupita took her world literature class to the Maya bookmaking workshop, Ronald held his computer out in front of him to record the blessing ceremony. Other people, of course, photographed Ronald photographing the shaman. I had decided long ago to leave my camera at home. Marcey had told me she stopped photographing the Maya when it became clear they viewed it as intrusive. She turned to street photography, giving community shows that her subjects attended. It was a fifty-year evolutionary process. Ronald was at the beginning stages. I hoped he would live to evolve. His suicidal moment came when he straddled the center line of the Pan-American Highway and did a little dance to his iTunes. He swayed left just as a truck materialized, missing him. He then rolled right, unaware. He was wearing his headphones and looking at the sky.

"Someone pulled him out of the road, but he kept his earphones on," Lupita told me. "I saw the whole thing through the window of the bus."

Ronald was, of course, fascinated by Brittany—the unattainable, for Ronald. It must have been difficult, because the rest of the students were getting sex constantly. Kevin, in particular, had a hard time returning to his homestay frequently enough to get his underwear washed. He would be on his way home at 3:00 a.m. and get pulled into a private party. School was at 9:00 a.m., so Kevin started looking more and more crumpled as the week went on. Was this the same person as the tentative young man at the Marietta coffeehouse?

None of the families complained about the carousing, and the town itself just folded the students into its expectations. Aside from alcohol poisoning and STDs, they really couldn't hurt themselves. Their behavior did create a rift, however, with the people trying to have a studious experience. By the time we got to the field trip at the end of the month, the wild bunch and the civilized bunch weren't speaking. To get to the town of Palenque, we took a tortuous seven-hour bus ride, which we broke up to swim under the fifty-foot waterfall at Misol-Há. The following morning, with Carol Karasik, our archaeoastronomer poet guide, we floated down the crocodile-infested Usumacinta River—the border with Guatemala—toward the ruins at Yaxchilán and Bonampak.

"It's an old story of political intrigue in the seventh century," Carol began, "over the legacy of Shield Jaguar and Lady Xoc, his wife. It's a pretty strange love story. She, a noblewoman from a powerful Yaxchilán family, performs a blood sacrifice in honor of the birth of the king's heir—born of a foreign princess, Lady Evening Star of Calakmúl. But Shield Jaguar ignores Lady Evening Star in the monuments. The heir, Bird Jaguar, later honors his mother by building a temple for her. Then he marries and publicly acknowledges a local noblewoman, Lady Great Skull Zero. It's the only site where we see so many women performing bloodletting ceremonies and having visions—and kings acknowledging their political debts to local and foreign-born queens."

I was her audience of one, the students being busy using the temples as jungle gyms. We left quite a few students by the pool at the hotel, their first return to North American luxury. They were beyond archaeological caviar at this point. Suddenly, we heard an extended psychotic scream.

One of the African American students had been eating a banana while standing before the maze tunnels, and a bat flew out of the dark and got tangled in her hair. At that moment, she lost her mind. Lupita told me that a blank-eyed, screaming zombie vectored directly at her.

"David tackled her to the ground before she hit me," Lupita said.

Back at the hotel in Palenque, we learned Brittany was still sick with giardia, a common water-borne infection, so we hiked to a pharmacy for meds.

"No drinking with these," we said.

The morning came, and we all packed up to meet Carol at the Palenque ruins, except for Brittany, who was not ambulatory. Her roommate wasn't speaking to her but told me Brittany had been drinking as usual the night before. I called the hotel doctor, who for $100 gave her a shot. She decided she could sleep on the bus while we went to the ruins, and, an hour late for our rendezvous with Carol, we got on the road.

When we arrived at the ruins, Brittany, having bounced back, hopped off with the others. Of course, only about three of the students stuck with Carol as she took us through the equinox alignments of the buildings and the politics of Palenque then and now. Kevin, in particular, had disappeared.

"They are the worst I've ever seen," said Carol. "Not even high schoolers. And that girl yesterday with the bat."

By the time we arrived at the museum, Kevin was still missing, and time was becoming a problem. The bus drivers were having a strike and had blocked the highway between Palenque and Villa-hermosa, where we were planning to spend the night before flying out the next day. We would have to take a five-hour detour to get around them. We waited for an hour, and still no Kevin. I walked up the road in time to see him pop out of the jungle with his ear-flapped hat, obviously pleased with himself.

He had been swinging from the trees like Tarzan, like an anthropologist. "Fer-de-lance," I said. "The deadliest snake in the world. That's why you stay on the paths." Carol had told me about the snakes, and I remembered that the first time I came to Palenque, someone found one on the path.

"One of them fell off my roof and landed on my head," Carol said. "They just told me, 'Put it out of your mind.' And Susan Prince had one fall on her head, too. She kind of leaned back as it went down her face. She later choreographed a dance about it. We went shopping for snaky fabric for her costume."

All the students plugged in their iPods and slept through our detour, through the rolling hilled cattle country with grand-mothers sewing on porches and swimming holes full of children. Lupita and I took it in. Rural Mexico, slow and savory.

"The pool at the hotel we're going to," I told her, "has three levels overlooking the city. I've been thinking about it for days."

"Can't wait," she said. "We deserve it."

Our bus pulled up to the Villahermosa Hilton, near the air-port. Lupita and I were handing out room keys when we noticed Brittany sitting in the hall, crying. Her bag had not made it onto the bus in Palenque—her bag with her passport inside it. I thought about the bag piles I had seen outside the bus and her roommate's pissed-off expression.

"Just go to your room," I said. "I'll get a taxi to bring the bag."

"Those Mexicans are going to steal my passport," she said.

"They're not stealing mine," I said, meanly. "Now why do you think that is?"

I called the hotel in Palenque, and because we had stayed there for the past three years, they convinced a taxi driver to take the chance on being paid when he delivered Brittany's bag. The drivers' strike had cleared up, so he wouldn't have to take an all-night detour. As it was, another $100 went on Brittany's IOU.

The sun was going down as I joined the students in the three-tier pool. The ugly city of Villahermosa was bathed in golden light, and the brimming water slid to the edge of the drop-off like the cliff pools in the sierra, only safe and man-made. We had our moment here, of evaporation off skin and caress of Gulf wind. On a tip from the well-mannered students, Lupita and I decided to grill Brittany later about bringing drugs through customs. We would walk on through. If they stopped her, we weren't turning back.

At the airport, Brittany commandeered a wheelchair, but none of her party buddies would help her. Only Ronald had his moment and wheeled her, like a wounded eagle, through the terminal.

Despite one of the students leaving her passport on the connecting flight to Houston, everyone but Kevin made it home safely to Atlanta. He had decided to stay behind in Mexico. Lupita and I would run into him again a year later while connecting in Houston, and Carol would report sighting him in Palenque. He now lives in Mexico and is a professor there. Brittany also went back, after a trip through Italy, deciding San Cristóbal was the best place in the world. I even returned the following year, after swearing I would never travel with students again.

Rebozo Caramelo, Santa María del Río, San Luis Potosí, 2002. Backstrap-
loomed silk ikat, 106 × 25 in. Private collection.

Travels with Betty

Mexico City, July 2010

"*REBOZOS FINOS,*" MY friend Ambar Past, poet and founder of the Maya bookmaking collective Taller Leñateros, said. "They're from Tenancingo. We went there on the bus." She was wearing a fine cotton ikat rebozo that I hadn't seen in cotton in Santa María del Río. I had seen them in Morelia, but perhaps Tenancingo was the source. Women who love weaving too much are always seeking the eye of the water, where the spring comes from deep out of the earth. I was on my way to visit Betty, the artist, in Mexico City.

"OK," I thought. "Betty and I can find it."

After I put the students on the plane home from Chiapas, I took a cab to Betty and Pepe's house in Coyoacán, the historic suburb where Frieda Kahlo once lived. "Oh my God," she said upon seeing me, and she immediately booked a massage for me around the corner. "How were they this year?"

"Still trying to drown themselves in margarita glasses," I said. Those huge round cocktails now reminded me of swimming pools, although there was a time I wouldn't have noticed.

My troubles with the students paled beside the troubles now

afflicting Mexico, which were spread out for us in yellow journalism in the morning paper Pepe was reading.

"Ambulance ambushed in Cuidad Juárez. Narcos to blame," he said.

"They're shooting up ambulances?"

"Now Mexico City has become the new safe place," Pepe said. "It's ironic after all these years."

Pepe, as a conservationist, ignored all the news and traveled constantly, saving wetlands and butterflies and establishing ecological reserves. This also meant he wasn't going to advise Betty to stay home.

We hopped in her Nissan and negotiated the one-way alleys in Coyoacán, avoiding the spillover from the zocalo, which had been taken over by street vendors. It was great for tourists but annoying for people who wanted to sit in their own park. As we were driving through San Ángel, Betty pointed out the house of a friend who discovered her neighbors ran a narco safe house when the police broke down their door in the middle of the night. It was an ivy-covered, upper-class neighborhood on a cobblestone street.

Tenancingo lay to the southwest, so we headed for Toluca on the highway. You have to climb out of Mexico City to the west, over the pine-wooded mountains. Toluca is high, perched over the drop-off. We took city streets to find the market, where Betty thought we could inquire about rebozos finos. All along the streets strings of green sausage hung in window jambs and doorways. It was the local specialty, like the famous tortas de Malpaso chorizo sandwich of the North. Since we were there, Betty headed for a place I usually avoided in the market, the meat section. No refrigeration, strips of meat hung from racks, yellow chickens with feet protruding out into the aisles, lots of interested flies, thin sheets of *carne adobada*—red meat slathered with red chile—insides of pigs, and, yes, green chorizo sausages in abundance. Fearlessly, Betty ordered several slabs of carne adobada and the chorizo. Taking the paper bag back to the car, she tossed it into the trunk, where it remained for the rest of the day.

Rebozos were not to be found in the *artesanía* section, but we were directed to another town further toward the coast. Signs for pyramids marked its outskirts, and we dropped down on the wooded highway. We saw the sign for Tenango and made the turn, headed for a town up on a hill, the church steeple dominating the valley. It was getting to be afternoon. No, this was not the rebozo town, we learned, and meanwhile Betty noticed street vendors selling blue corn empanadas, one of her favorites. The rough stone-ground exterior held spicy potatoes, so that even one empanada was rather hard to get through. Did I mention that I was recovering from typhoid, which I had contracted in Chiapas from eating salad at Ambar's house? She did not believe in stainless-steel sinks, preferring the wooden Maya ones that looked like miniature canoes. Scary food was turning out to be a recurring motif. Still, eating street food in the noon sun in the high plateau town, with the white walls and red tiles and blooming jacaranda, was like taking a bite of the day. The cumin made its way up my nose. I leaned against Betty's car. The empanada lady smiled and took our tinfoil wrappings.

Sustained, we continued back to the highway and lost another thousand feet before we found Tenancingo. Indeed it was the home to rebozos finos, many shops now closed for siesta, but the market was open, and stall after stall was filled with fine ikat cotton rebozos with hand-knotted fringe, the longer the more expensive. As usual, I went for a conservative black and white, while Betty ventured into a stunning turquoise-and-black shawl that screamed Southwest, which was where she was from. She came from an old Arizona ranching family, which explained why she was unafraid to drive in the Mexico City traffic.

"Well," she told me, "when I was four my mother put me on a horse and said, 'Go get in the cows.'" It explained a lot.

Rebozos in hand, we could now amble back to the city, taking a scenic route. It was rush hour when we hit the *periférico*, the highway that circles the city, and dark by the time we arrived in Coyoacán. I had forgotten all about the green chorizo, now in the trunk eight hours.

Betty opened her Coldspot stainless-steel refrigerator and extracted tortillas and things to chop for tacos. While Pepe fussed over their dog Mira's croquets, Betty threw the carne adobada on the block and the green chorizo, and with the burnt chile and spices permeating the room, we sat at the kitchen bar, talked politics and religion, and ate taco after taco, the Toluca fame truly earned in the most delicious green chorizo this side of, well, Malpaso.

Ixmiquilpan, July 2010

The following summer, I was interested in the Otomí homeland, and Betty was interested in getting her soap and toiletries holder replaced, and so we headed for Ixmiquipan, where she remembered buying it. The structure was made of cane, or *carrizo*, and was two stories, open at the front like a dollhouse, with little rooms that held things. Being cane, it could take humidity and water, so it was perfect for a bathroom. Betty had had it for about twenty years. Ixmiquilpan was in Hidalgo, the next state to the north from Mexico City, in the Mexquital Valley, full of the huge agave cacti that provided the ixtle fibers used to weave bags, tablecloths, and, formerly, clothing. The Otomís I had met in San Pablito also had a homeland there.

We started in the market, asking around. We found shops with miniature cedar instruments inlaid with abalone and mother-of-pearl. We found boxes with inlay. Sombreros of palm, Otomí manta tablecloths with yarn-embroidered animals. No carrizo soap holders. We had almost given up when someone in a shop directed us to a workshop on a side street. There they made things out of carrizo.

"Would you like to look at the book of possibilities?" the carrizo artist asked us.

Turning the pages, Betty found her very dollhouse and placed an order.

Later, I asked her, "So you knew that even after twenty years you would find them still doing this?"

"I didn't know, but I was hoping."

Tecolutla, Veracruz, July 2011

After the summer of 2011 with the students in Oaxaca, Betty put me in her Nissan, and we headed toward the Gulf and El Tajín. Betty had forgotten her map, so we got lost in Ecatepec briefly. We soon found the highway again, and with the pyramids of Teotihuacán on our left, we drove through the eastern mountains that dropped off down to the ocean. We stopped on top to eat breakfast and to see if they had any preserved chile. The restaurant, constructed entirely out of knotty pine, overlooked a dam and had local products for sale: honey, jams, and little souvenirs.

Soon it was all downhill. We passed the turnoff for El Tajín, an enigmatic archaeological site that turned out to be all ball courts.

Perhaps an Olympic Games site for Mesoamericans. Odd niches and Hopi storm cloud–like designs. We did not stop, submersion in the ocean being our goal. Following the river, the land flattened out into an alluvial plain. The town at the end of the road was Tecolutla, a very Mexican beach resort. I had been at so many resorts based on the North American model that this little town was a welcome relief. We found a small hotel just down the dirt road from the beach and soon, in flip-flops and bathing suits, found ourselves on a flat beach with palapas and beach chairs perched on the water's edge. We rented chairs and ran into the calm, tepid surf. Free at last.

As the afternoon progressed, more and more of the town's inhabitants came down to the beach, some in bathing suits, some just in their street clothes. After getting wet, they sat down in beach chairs and proceeded to enjoy the main attraction in Tecolutla: food carts. The hard Gulf sand provided an ideal roadway for vendors of cold coconuts with straws, alcoholic beverages, Mexico City–style tacos, oysters, seafood cocktails, beachwear (in a large Fellini-esque wagon, top-heavy and listing from side to side), salted nuts, regional sweets, snow cones, crepes, roasted corn on the cob, pancakes with *dulce de leche* topping, fried fish, and soft drinks. After watching one young woman make shrimp cocktails nonstop from one end of the beach to the other, we decided to nosh.

"She washes her hands after every cocktail," Betty said. "And she's gone through three bags of fresh shrimp and is getting more."

"Sounds like our best bet," I said. "*Campechanas,*" seafood cocktails.

"Oysters," Betty said, observing that a relative of Pepe's had died from eating oysters on the beach at Veracruz. She slurped one out of its pearly shell. Mexico makes one feel so alive, on a daily basis. Right up there with railroading.

After recovering from the cocktails, more surf, then more noshing. The food carts sailed their course all afternoon, until the shadows of the beach umbrellas grew long and families packed up and headed back to their houses. It was a great way to get through the doggy heat of the afternoon, and now that the sun was off the roofs, they could nap and get ready to eat again later, when the town had cooled. We joined the citizens after dark, vendors selling clothing and shell bracelets now set up on the sidewalks and in the plaza. After making our *vuelta*, or turn around the park, we settled on an open-air fish restaurant well patronized by the locals and ate *huachinango a la Jarocho*, red snapper Veracruz style, sautéed in tomatoes, chile, and olives. As we strolled back to our little hotel, the full moon rising in the humid air was our own fullness and content.

Glancing over my shoulder, something sharklike caught my attention. "Betty," I said, "keep walking. Don't turn around."

On the quiet street, the first of a line of squat mobile tanks passed us, with ski-masked soldiers alert behind their mounted machine guns. The whole silent squadron passed us and turned the corner. I noticed they had traffic cones with them.

"Out to blockade the Zetas on the road?" I wondered. I had been reading the papers again.

"Who knows?" Betty said. "But it certainly puts a damper on."

"Why do they all look fifteen?"

"Because they are."

Ranulfo Hernández, Deer, San Martín Tilcajete, Oaxaca, 2000.
Wood, 14 × 9 × 3.5 in. Private collection.

An Ear and a Tail

Oaxaca City, June 2012

THE WALL OF kudzu and wisteria was weaving itself again, in a
Georgia spring, as I turned left at the estate sale sign. My Marietta
neighborhood of old Edwardian cottages saw many estate sales as
the older residents died and the new, young gentry moved in.
Lush lawns, azalea hedges, gazing balls, and angel lawn statues—I
braced myself for the sense of sadness I often felt entering. This
house, however, was filled with folk art, thousands of objects—
faux primitive painted boards, lots of cheap Chinese pottery,
moldy weaving, miniatures, painted crockery, wooden fowl—but
nothing inspiring joy.

Then a flash of familiar color as two shoppers seized upon a
Mexican deer I knew to be from Oaxaca, the one vital object in the
sea of sameness. They had left me another, a blue deer with mauve
paisley spots, missing an ear and a tail, the Oaxacan carvers making protuberances removable for easy packing. I turned it over and
read the carver's name, Ranulfo Hernández. He was from San
Martín Tilcajete, Oaxaca. I wondered if the collectors had gone to
Oaxaca to buy this or if it had made its way to a museum show or
a Costco display. It seemed unlikely that they had traveled all the

way to San Martín, a sleepy carvers' village thirty minutes outside of Oaxaca City on the road to the Pacific Coast. Since I was going there in a few months with my summer students in tow, I thought I would look up the carver and ask for new appendages. Georgia had been experiencing a wave of immigration from Mexico, and as a transplant from Santa Cruz, I was glad to see the migrants. The deer reminded me of home and light and the western mountains in California, places I could now only visit and not live in.

There were three main carving towns near Oaxaca City: San Antonio Arrazola, where Manuel Jiménez started the carving craze using copal woodl; San Martín Tilcajete; and La Unión. The folk art trade routes to the US Southwest galleries popularized the carvings, called "alebrijes," after their original form in papier-mâché from Pedro Linares López in Mexico City. Now a substantial number of artists in these towns made a living from carving, although the market was giving way to wholesalers, who offered the artists much less than retail. I had visited San Martín in 1992, when only a dirt road led into the town, off the highway served by second-class buses from Oaxaca. Every household, it had seemed then, was carving, with all family members busy making giraffes one day, and dreamed outer-space monsters the next. The town itself was in the flat agricultural valley, with adobe houses and ocotillo fences, herds of goats being driven through the streets, and plowed fields fronting the road in. Then I had visited the Fuentes family, Epifanio famous in *Smithsonian* magazine for his angels with long, flowing ixtle hair. I bought a blue mermaid from him and a pink angel carved by his brother, Alejandrino, and took it back to Santa Cruz with me. I brought the angel home in a basket, and the nose was damaged. Not long after, I saw an article in the local paper on Florencio Fuentes, a carver from San Martín, who was in Santa Cruz working. Yes, he was related, and I took him the angel, and he repaired it.

Now, twenty years later, with the summer students in language school in Oaxaca City, I took a bus out to the San Martín turnoff. The road in had been paved for a few years now, and three-wheel mini-taxis operated to and from the center. I started asking for Ranulfo.

"Oh no," another carver told me, "he is not here now. But his in-laws live here, just down that street."

I knocked on the in-laws' big sheet-metal gate. A man in his eighties opened the door and introduced himself as Raúl Fabián Cisneros.

"Hi," I said. "I am looking for the carver who made this deer. I would like him to repair it."

He invited me into the courtyard, and his wife, Francisca Mendoza Aguilar, brought out plastic chairs, so we could sit under the guaje tree, and a pitcher of water.

"We have not seen him, or our daughter Ana, for twelve years," Raul said. "They left with our grandchildren to work. He works in a hotel, but I don't know which one. He is in Santa Cruz, California. They called this morning, but we don't call them."

"Of course he was," I thought. The net of connections I traveled within amazed me. I fished out the remaining ear. They examined it.

"It needs a tail also," I said.

Francisca brought out a binder of photographs, an album of Ranulfo's work. We found my blue deer. I told them I was writing a story about finding it at the estate sale and the connections between the States and Mexico and that I came often to Oaxaca with students. I could feel the regret in both of them, although they were, in the Mexican manner, hospitable with me, a stranger who had just parachuted into their home with this improbable story. Who was I, after all? I knew how hard it was for Mexicans to travel to the United States, starting with the journey to Mexico City for visas and the bank account requirements, not to mention that their purpose would be to visit undocumented workers who had no legal right to be in the United States themselves. And yet it was peaceful under the tree and in their swept dirt yard with the flowers and fruit, the animals, and village life all around them. I envied them their location, yet their pain was obvious. I gave them my university business card to reassure them and asked that they give the e-mail address to Ranulfo, although I knew I would have to contact him. After thirty-four years in Santa Cruz, I had a feeling I could find him. Oddly, both of us had been in exile working elsewhere for about the same length of time.

The following March, on my spring break, I flew to Santa Cruz. My old friend Amy Locks, who was married to someone I had worked with on the railroad, was an immigration lawyer. I asked her if she knew any workers from Oaxaca. "Only about a hundred," she said. She made a call, and her informant made ten calls, and within a day I had Ranulfo's phone and address, with a recommendation from a fellow worker. I called him and introduced myself as the person who had visited his in-laws.

"Oh yes," he said. "They said someone came, asking for me." We made a date for Amy and me to visit.

Ranulfo lived in a Oaxacan enclave in an apartment in Capitola, a beach town down the coast. His son Gerardo, fourteen, opened the door and asked us in to wait. His son Daniel, eighteen, was watching TV with his sister Keyna, ten. Amy started asking Daniel about his history and was able to tell him he would qualify for the DREAM Act, which enabled children who came to the United States illegally to obtain citizenship. She handed out her card. She was such a great lawyer and person that I thought,

"Well, at least they get to meet her out of all of this." Soon Ranulfo and Ana, holding their nine-month-old baby, Juliana, came back from the store.

Ranulfo was *chaparrito*, short, as they say affectionately in Oaxaca, and when I produced the ear and described the deer, his smile appeared and my visit seemed to make sense to him. I called him "maestro," or teacher, out of respect and told him I was a writer working on a story about the coincidence of finding the deer and knowing where it came from and that it could be a symbol for migration and that I, in a much less radical way, was a migrant for work myself. He was working as a janitor in a hotel, and Ana was working as a maid. Dani had just graduated from high school. I wondered what they felt about their past lives as artisans.

"One person had the dream," he said, "then the rest followed. Alebrijes come from the imagination. This beauty," he paused, "is necessary for life."

He held out his hands to show me the scars the knife had left, the cost of his art. He went into the kitchen and came back with a photograph of a child on the floor in a sea of wooden iguanas. It was Dani as a boy in Oaxaca. Their life as artisans began when they were eighteen, he carving and Ana independently learning to decorate the figures. They lived with the in-laws and made the figures there, where I had visited. After a while they opened a tin-roofed stand on the main street and tried to live by their art, but tourist sales fell off, and the wholesalers came and offered the equivalent of $300 for a lot. Then they followed the road to Santa Cruz, taken by so many of their neighbors.

Talking about carving, Ranulfo transformed, and he agreed to make me a new ear and tail.

"It would be good to have the copal wood, about this much," he said, indicating a foot-long piece, "and green if possible." He was confident I could deliver it.

"Of course," I said. "I will bring it after the summer."

"I miss my parents," Ana said. "They are old, and we can talk on the phone, and the children will be able to visit them someday, but it is not the same as holding someone in your arms." She was holding Juliana as she spoke.

When I went to Oaxaca the next summer with the students, I remembered that image of Ana, and I could not bring myself to visit her parents in San Martín. It seemed obscene to me that I could go visit them and she could not. But I went to San Martín with the students, where we made our usual stop at the house of Jacobo Angeles, one of the most famous carvers. The students always loved seeing Jacobo show them the colors that could be made from plants and how adding something like lemon juice could change a color. Jacobo trained young carvers and painters, who were seated at long tables working on alebrijes. His more elaborate pieces sold for thousands of dollars in galleries in the States.

"Of course I know Ranulfo," he said. "I am the godfather to Dani and Keyna. What a small world. I would be happy to send him some copal wood." His assistant cut off part of a trunk of the green wood. I was already wondering how I would carry it back, reminding me of Leon Panetta's alabaster owls.

"Do many people from here go there?" I asked.

"All the time," he said. "My two cousins just left yesterday."

Our next stop was the studio of Vicente Hernández Vásquez, whose irreverent sense of humor led him to carve devils on the cross and riding motorcycles, among other nightmares. When I asked him why a devil would be on a cross—I bought two of them—he giggled maniacally. He also gave me a more modest branch of green copal for his countryman Ranulfo. Santa Cruz and San Martín were starting to seem closer. In fact, one of the things I found comforting in Mexico was that I could always walk home.

That same summer we visited the studio of another successful Oaxacan artist, Alejandro Santiago, who was from Teococuilco de Marcos Pérez, a small mountain town above Oaxaca City. Alejandro went to Paris to study and made a name for himself as a painter and sculptor. But upon returning to his pueblo, he missed the friends who had left to work in the United States—so many that Teococuilco de Marcos Pérez, like numerous others in the state of Oaxaca, became a town of women, children, and old people. The young men were gone. Alejandro then crossed the border illegally himself to understand the experience and was arrested and deported. He remembered seeing thousands of crosses painted on the border walls, representing those who had died crossing. So Alejandro started his *migrantes* project, replacing the lost migrants with 2,501 life-sized fired clay figures he planned to exhibit in various stages of the journey to the border. The 2,501st migrant figure was himself.

I had brought another group of students to his art farm in Santiago Suchilquitongo in 2006, the year the teachers' strike took over the city for six months. He was still creating the migrants in walk-in kilns, firing at temperatures of 2,000 degrees. The kiln barn was full of silent clay Zapotec men and women, naked, assembled, and waiting. He was eventually able to have exhibitions, but the planned route to the border became too dangerous in the exploding cartel violence. When we visited the art farm this time, the migrants had become miniaturized and packable. The barn was now full of dwarves.

The road to Santiago Suchilquitongo left the highway to Mexico

City and turned from asphalt to dirt. As soon as we left the *carretera*, time slowed down, as did our van. It was sandy river-bottom land, carrizo lining the water bank and nopal and ocotillo forming the borders of the fields. We could now feel the intense tropical sun and breathe in the smells it released in the air. This sensual air was the drug of rural Mexico, as potent as marijuana. We passed every form of transportation on the road: old cars, trucks with people riding in the back, boys on horseback, men walking behind herds of goats and cattle, people on bicycles, two men riding an oxcart drawn by oversized Brahman cattle, women with water jars or loads of wrapped laundry balanced on their heads. We overshot the dirt path turnoff to the art farm, since there was no sign or name, just a distinctive clump of carrizo marking a fork in the road. We came to a gate and honked the horn. After a while, a worker walked down the long driveway leading to the ranch house and motioned us through. The grasses were tall in the fronting fields, and a slight breeze alternately revealed and concealed the clay migrants sleeping in the pasture, all of them, like a Chinese emperor's city of the dead, slowly returning to the earth.

"Oh my God," I thought, "what can the students make of this?"

Alejandro died the following summer of a heart attack, following his migrants into the earth.

Arte Amuzgo is a small storefront on Cinco de Mayo Street in Oaxaca City. The backstrap-woven textiles inside are from the Amusgo villages in the Mixteca Alta region in the mountains to the northwest. I think of this store as an art gallery, filled with tactile paintings. The garments represent months and months of work by the weavers in the cooperative, who use three wooden sticks and their bodies to create tension on the portable backstrap looms. The cotton is hand grown, dyed with natural dyes, and hand spun. When I first saw Amusgo dresses twenty years ago, only the center panel was fantastically brocaded. Now the huipils have all three panels, front and back, completely brocaded with gradated colors.

In the summer of 2013, the owner of the shop, Odilón Merino Morales, an indigenous weaver from San Pedro Amuzgos, was invited to show the textiles at the annual International Folk Art Market in Santa Fe, New Mexico. My friend Martha Sorensen accompanied him on a flight from Oaxaca through Houston. He had his import papers, his temporary visa, his invitation to present at the show—everything, including two fifty-pound bags full of handmade textiles. He was unlucky with his immigration agent, an American of Hispanic descent. This man held him up for two hours, saying things like, "This is a country with laws" and "You're an *Indio*, and you're just here to break the laws and make money, and we're going to stop you." The agent demanded to know why he was wearing a beaded mandala.

"I am Indian," Odilón replied. "It is my culture to wear things like this."

Along with his only copy of his inventory list, the agent confiscated his textiles, even though Odilón had paid $800 in import duty, so that Odilón did not have them for the all-important first night sale to wealthy shoppers who could afford to pay $1,500 each to attend. The agent also red flagged his visa; now every time he came to the United States he would face a similar interrogation. Martha was not allowed to wait for him, and when she met him after the ordeal, she said, "He was white as a sheet." And he is not white, clearly the problem to begin with. But then, neither was the immigration agent.

"He was afraid to fly in the first place," Martha said, "and now he says he will never do it again. He took the bus home, two days, with some other artists, so that he wouldn't have to."

The organizers of the International Folk Art Market intervened through their customs brokers and rescued his wares, but otherwise, he would have spent his organization's money in vain. They have invited him back for next year, but he is hesitating.

"You could fly to Juárez," I said, "and avoid Houston completely. Then cross the border, and Martha could pick you up in El Paso." He brightened up. He would only have to fly in Mexico.

"Considering that trade has been going on for over a thousand years for turquoise from the Southwest to Tututepec," I added, "it seems to me you have a perfect right to continue it." Tututepec was the Mixtec port trading city very near San Pedro Amuzgos.

"That's right," he responded. "I want to go there and bring my son, so he can see what his history is. I know we are connected, because I can read it in the designs."

I have bought textiles from his little store in Oaxaca City several times. I have two huipils made from the Amusgo open-weave rebozos, crocheted together to make a new-style blouse. Indigenous fashions are continually evolving in response to demand from foreign and upper-class Mexican purchasers. I hold my breath before going into the store, because the textiles are priced fairly and they cost many hundreds of dollars. The color combinations and the subtle brocades imitate nature's ability to manifest color. The weavers' skill can come only with isolation and lack of work options. The outreach by markets such as Oaxaca City, Mexico City, and Santa Fe can reward the weavers enough to keep these art forms in production. Otherwise, they will be gone, along with the disappearing languages. Dress and language are the only possessions of some indigenous cultures.

"I am ashamed of my country for treating you like this," I told him. "I would like to think it was only that one man."

But then I remembered coming back from Huatulco with my colleague Lupita and her Mexican-born but US citizen mother, who had just had two hip replacements. There was no wheelchair available at the gate in Houston, in spite of the fact that we had requested one in advance. They "ran out." So Juana had to hobble the long distance to the immigration line, where, because she looks very Mexican, she was taken into a room and interrogated. Since she had a tight connection to make, we were worried, but we were not allowed to wait for her anywhere near the immigration checkpoint. Agents yelled at us to "move on." As Martha was yelled at when she tried to wait for Odilón.

People immigrate illegally because there are no sustainable jobs for them in Mexico. US seniors, meanwhile, are crossing the border for affordable medical care or housing. People cross the border with drugs from Mexico or with guns from the United States. Why artists with traditional handcrafts and legal visas should be excessively scrutinized is a mystery to me. Perhaps they are just an easy target, like mothers.

Ranulfo, by the way, has succeeded in getting his papers to live legally in the United States. I sent the copal wood to Amy Locks, who had it in the trunk of her car when she ran into Ana at Orchard Supply Hardware in Santa Cruz. Ranulfo now has the wood, and I am still waiting for the ear and tail. It will get to me if God wills it.

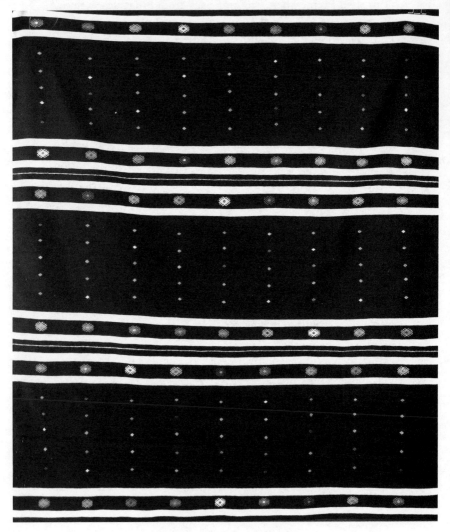

Benita López López, Mantel Estrella, Bayalemho, San Andrés Larráinzar, Chiapas, 2015. Backstrap-loomed cotton, 47 × 45 in. Private collection.

Shopping

Oaxaca City, June 2015

I TUCKED THE students into their homestays and hit MARO, the women artisans' cooperative, looking for shirts and a lighter version of Matl design by Matilde Poulat earrings. Nothing much new there. Then I stopped in Cielito Lindo, an upscale store on the tourist street, to see if they had any Guadalajara manta blouses, as well as Xquenda and the other stores that carried them. Manta is manufactured muslin, often elaborated by hand. Nope—the new styles were thicker and less interesting than what I wanted. Rebozos were innovative last year, but this year there was nothing much around. ARIPO, a state-run crafts store, was geriatric, with textiles looking as if they weren't moving at all. I tried the Benito Juárez market, the row of artesenía clothing stalls. Still many copies of Remigio Mestas Revilla's standard manta blouse in garish colors that would run all over your washing machine. A few storefronts occupied by the sellers who used to set up booths in the zocalo carried copies of Odilón's rebozo turned blouse at slightly lower prices, but without his color sense. They also had copies of Remigio's blouse. Sierra Morena had manta from Guadalajara, but it was shopworn. They had lots of dress-length Tuxtepec embroidered rayon blouses and Huave huipils in a variety of colors, a la Remigio, but the weaving was coarse. "OK," I thought, "I have to go to the source," and I went into Los Baúles de Juana Cata, Remigio's store.

This place was a sanctuary for high-end, educated shoppers. Remigio Mestes named his store The Trunks of doña Cata for the impresario Juana C. Romero, the friend of President Portfirio Díaz who introduced velvet and silk thread to Tehuantepec. Remigio's adoptive mother and grandmother, Mari Cruz and Delores, had their own store around the corner, an institution with the opposite approach to Remigio's. Their store resembled a bazaar where you had to paw through stacks of clothing to find a treasure, all the while hectored by a pressured salesperson.

"What can I show you?"

"Hard to tell," I said, looking at the piles. What did I want in here? Something, but . . .

Remigio knew his shoppers. They wanted to see treasures right away. Lots of them. Kiss your wallet good-bye, ye who enter here. Remigio's trunks were filled with sweet-smelling textiles from all the regions of Oaxaca, where he traveled and placed orders, supplying the high-quality thread. Natural fibers, natural colors, subdued and sophisticated palettes, and all washed in a distinctive soap so the weavers could tell which items were laundered. The odor also acted as a memory release that transported shoppers back in time, to where? Perhaps into the nostalgia that drew them to Mexico, a place that seemed to be reminiscent, if not of their own pasts, then of a past they wished to have. I was reminded of the genius trade name of Design Within Reach.

There were newer boutiques in Oaxaca now that modeled the completely upper-class shopping experience of paying for pure idea, the textiles themselves not embodying countless hours of hand labor. "Yes, I have tons of frivolous money to throw away," their customers might think. Not in this store. You were paying for art and tradition combined. But you had to know a lot to understand the relative value of what you were buying.

So I forked over $140 for a sweet-smelling *quechquemitl*, or triangular blouse, from the Zapotecs of San Juan Tagui. In lavender gray and indigo blue. Of a gossamer thread and hand-sewn, cross-stitched seams in cotton thread dyed the matching colors.

Still reeling, I thought, "Why not check the Museo Textil de Oaxaca, which Remigio had helped set up, to see if they had any other colors in his less expensive manta line?"

Normally, I wouldn't have spoken to the American woman in the textile museum. American shoppers like to be left alone, an experience you can't have in Mexico apart from the big-box stores like Gigante or, now, Walmart. I was in rescue mode, however, from taking care of the students. So when the woman asked the clerk, who did not speak English, whether the wool quechquemitl she was looking at was alpaca, I unthinkingly answered her.

"No, it's sheep's wool," I said. "*Churras*—they don't use alpaca here."

I heard an intake of breath. She was holding back from biting me. Or maybe she would bite me. She wasn't sure. She had a very short haircut, spiked and highlighted blonde. She was about my age. She wore raw linen three-quarter-length pants, an Eileen Fisher tunic, a matching raw linen scarf, Think sandals, round titanium glasses, and an expensive watch. She carried the antithesis power bag, a hemp sack.

"Thank you," she said. It meant, "Fuck you."

The unwanted tourist in her solitary dream, I excused myself and left. But had I seen myself in the mirror?

As I walked back to the hotel, I passed other American

shoppers on a mission. They did not greet, eyes down, blanking me out of the picture. It was important that they be alone, shopping. I thought, "God. Am I like that? Well, at least I speak Spanish."

I looked at what I was wearing and thought about how much it had cost: Ralph Lauren jeans from eBay. Keen sandals. Hello Kitty watch. A fancy manta blouse from the Guadalajara maker Dunes. An oilcloth shopping bag from the market. Total price, $200. Still a month's wages for a daily worker. One of Remigio's blouses would cost the equivalent.

I started noticing. A dark shadow crossing the street, skinny jeans, $500 boots, Remigio's long, black manta blouse, big silver earrings, a $400 silk rebozo. Santa Fe style, and sure enough, meeting the shadow woman later, I learned she was on her way back there the next day. Remigio, like Odilón, was a participant in the Santa Fe International Folk Art Market. Here were his first-day sale shoppers, flying down for bargains and driving up real estate prices. Just what were we buying?

At the age of eight I became the kind of tourist I always would be when our family took the *Super Chief* train from Pasadena to Chicago to buy a new 1954 Oldsmobile in Detroit and drive it home over Route 66. I spent the first day of the trip shadowing an Indian guide I remembered as Sunshine, who loaded me down with postcards. His true name was Lowell Sun Rise, and he was from Zuni Pueblo. On the Santa Fe Railroad postcard he was wearing a red velvet shirt, a silver concha belt, two turquoise squash-blossom necklaces, two heavy turquoise bracelets, silver earrings, Kaibab moccasins, and a bandana head scarf.

I had been primed for this experience by living among stage sets for western movies, my birdwatcher father taking us to the outskirts of Los Angeles to look at the Mojave Desert and Borrego

Springs. When we drove home from Detroit, stopping at roadside trading posts, they bought me my first curio—an adult-sized, heavy, cast-silver belt buckle, with a turquoise deer in the center.

My taste was, and is, completely formed by the Santa Fe Railroad marketing department. That and reading the many naturalist books on the desert my father had in his library. So the three fashion items I have always owned are cowboy boots, Navajo moccasins, and turquoise jewelry. Of course, living five blocks from the annual Rose Parade, with the sheriff's posse palominos dripping with silver, didn't hurt either.

My father, a Caltech chemistry professor, had the Southwest as his recruiting territory, and so every spring he would visit high schools, interviewing promising young scientists. My mother would go sometimes and come home with souvenirs. They stayed at the Ghost Ranch Lodge in Tucson and brought back postcards and stories and Fred Harvey bracelets. And then there were the endless Kodacrome slides of empty desert, which we would watch at home. "Why is he taking pictures of sagebrush?" I wondered. "What is out there?"

What I absorbed was the idea of material culture, objects sheltering meaning. The Indian guides were on the train to talk about New Mexican Native culture and the landscape the train was traversing. Those links and the curiosity about them have never left me. As a migrant railroad brakeman in the Southwest, this dreamscape became real to me, and my romantic vision was replaced by experience. Working in Arizona, New Mexico, and Texas, I saw Mexican and Southwest culture objects, vibrant with embedded meaning, and I wondered about them. I collected them because they were alive to me. They had heat. Over the years, the authorship and the little tags saying who made each object have been lost in the chaos of my moving life, but these objects have been with me in railroad motel rooms, my temporary houses, and then in my home for the past sixteen years in the southeast, where their signs don't register with any but the migrants who are likewise seeking work here.

The spillover from my house is in my office at school: a life-sized straw mandrill from Mario López in Ihuátzio, textiles from Zinacantán and Lake Atitlán, Mazahua miniature weaving, and an embroidery of the Virgin of Guadalupe given to me by Juana, the woman from Guelatao de Juárez who sold gum on the street in Oaxaca City. Students don't know what to make of these things. "Wow," they say. "Your office is really different."

These objects have made it possible for me to live here, so far from home.

I wrote about shopping in *Boomer: Railroad Memoirs*, how it could substitute for the anxiety relievers— alcohol and drugs—I had previously used. When I first came to work in El Paso in 1983, I chose as a 12 Step sponsor a woman who introduced herself as a compulsive shopper and then sold me her brass bed to cover her credit card debt. I correctly figured she wouldn't give me a hard time about my shopping. Other people I know just window-shop in catalogs—I call it "catch and release," like fishermen who throw their fish back in the water. I think it is the oldest human pastime, to hunt and gather and then to trade. When in Mexico, I walk through the marketplace every day, notice what's new, and speak to people. When you participate in street life, people start to know you and expect you. When my friend Joanne Sterricker, a great shopper, came with me to study Spanish, the women from La Mixteca and the coast were selling weaving from their villages in booths set up for the Guelaguetza folk dance festival. Joanne bought many textiles, huipils made of naturally brown *coyuchi* cotton embroidered with shellfish-dyed thread and stained with the shellfish dye in splashes as patterns. With their rough texture and smell of the sea, the textiles were made over winter months and carried on the bus to the place of sale. The sellers romanced us, invited us to visit, and called to us as we passed on the street. In later years, when Joanne was not there, they always remembered her. "Where is your friend? *La grandota*, the big woman?"

I am reminded of Samuel Delany's memoir *Times Square Red, Times Square Blue*, in which he talks about the safety of being known on the street, when the street supported all classes of people and where he was greeted and watched over. When the street became gentrified, it was monochromatic, empty, and more dangerous.

There is an aspect of obsession to collecting. You start to learn the syntax of the objects, their histories, and you look for changes in style and material. You become the expert. You spot the natural brown dye masquerading as coyuchi or the imitation shellfish purple. As soon as I got to Oaxaca, I would check all the venues for what was new or from a region from which I didn't have a textile. I suppose it gave me an identity there, something to do, an identity both welcomed and resented.

As I wrote about shopping, I realized that there was no firm ground to stand on as a narrator. Should I look at my own identity as a tourist, traveler, guide, and shopper? As Carol Karasik, our archaeoastronomer poet guide in Palenque, asked me early on, "Are you a serious person or just a shopper?" Should I focus on the economics of the selling and buying exchange? The dream aspect of travel? The benefits and drawbacks of tourism? Tourist art contrasted with traditional art, and the various aspects of tradition? Or Native fashion, its conversation with itself? Jeans couture? Intersecting homes and migration? With any subject that has so many, often contradictory, faces, the discussion tends to mirror that fact. I have nothing definitive to say about shopping. It is like rain—too much is bad, too little is bad. But any woman I have traveled with in Chiapas has been very content to spend hours rooting through the weaving for sale in the market and willing to travel uncomfortably squished into a minivan to look for more in the villages. And the villagers, likewise, are happy to use cell phones, plastic slippers, acrylic cardigan sweaters, and cotton underwear.

I remember the first time I saw a knock-off of a Maya blouse from Aguacatenango in Chiapas. I was in a high-end dress store in Tucson. Biya, a division of Johnny Was, had knocked off the blouse design, had them produced in China, and was retailing them for $250. A Chiapas entrepreneur, not indigenous, had done a similar thing with authentically produced Aguacatenango blouses, dying them with natural dyes, aimed at high-end Mexican shoppers and foreigners who would be looking for natural dyes in a fashionable palette. I had bought these for $60, double their undyed retail price of $30—they were probably bought from their producers at $6. Women from Aguacatenango would approach me on the street and hard sell me the basic white muslin or satin variety for about $15. Biya could have had these blouses from their producers and sold them at a 250 percent markup, but in the global economy this is not enough, so they outsourced them for even more profit.

I buy works of art with money I earn working, but there is no per-hour equivalent. The tags on the textiles in the stores give the hours they took to weave, but hours are not relevant. The weaver is not guaranteed a forty-hour week, the basis for minimum wage in the United States. And then, one hour out of my eight-hour workday is not equivalent to one hour spent working at home with no commute, no eight- to twelve-hour exclusive commitment of time, no childcare expenses, the cost of living close to work, the buy-in to Social Security, Medicare, and insurance, not to mention that I had to relocate 2,000 miles and leave my home community for the job.

For the weaver, there is the ability to earn money working where she lives while caring for her children herself, raising her food in place, and walking everywhere in her community. Then there is the art factor, the ability to create beauty as she sees it and to engage in a sacred activity, which is priceless.

Where the two economies collide is in the cost of goods the producers need that they must buy. These things are subject to the inflation created by the operation of the money economy. So inflation, unless it consistently benefits the producers when they sell their product, depletes them since their cost of living goes up. To gain more power in the transactions, the indigenous producers organized into crafts cooperatives. As of the present, they still have not been able to give themselves more than a minimum wage of eight pesos per hour, or fifty US cents.

"Once they got organized to sell crafts, they got organized in everything," Carol Karasik said. The weavers then became able to effect change in other aspects of their lives, such as by negotiating power in their homes and communities. A French designer, Isabel Marant, ran afoul of an organized Oaxacan community, Santa María Tlahuitoltepec, in her 2015 summer Etoile collection, for which she appropriated the entire design of the typical blouse of that community. She did not credit the community for the design until another French company, Antik Batik, sued her over the same design, which they claimed was previously appropriated by them. But the idea of copyright or ownership of designs rests on the idea of sole authorship, not an idea that is native to a communal society. How can such a society lay legal claim to their intellectual property? Only through publicity, and the Internet is giving them that power. In a forum organized by the Museo Textil de Oaxaca, spokespeople from Tlahuitoltepec stated the blouse was "the collective heritage of indigenous people," that it was their identity that marked their place in the cosmos and an integral part of their belief system, and that its appropriation without credit was identity theft.

"The old tradition of wanting unique clothing for village identity goes way back, wanting to differentiate who belongs—identity," Eric Chávez Santiago, education director of the textile museum, told me. "Each community is different. Some only weave for themselves, some for sale. In Oaxaca, outsiders wearing the blouse does not imply disrespect. The communities that embrace sales are educated, not naïve, use the Internet, and are interested in adapting their traditions to induce buyers. Our museum goes to the communities and asks what they want. We speak their languages, and we offer help. We, for example, offer different kinds of cotton because there is only one type of cotton available here."

Before the 2015 Guelaguetza in Oaxaca, vendors set up their booths to sell their textiles. They slept in the booths for several weeks and sold directly to the public. I passed the booth from Tlahuitoltepec and spoke with Honorina Gómez Martínez, who was selling blouses. She had her mechanical sewing machine on the shelf to demonstrate that the designs were sewn by machine, but not a computerized one. It took her an eight-hour day to make one huipil, she told me. I bought a purple one with orange designs.

"What do you think of seeing a foreigner wearing one of your blouses, a person who obviously is not a member of your community?" I asked her.

"I feel proud," she said. "Do you want the skirt as well? For you," she went on, "the designs don't signify anything, but for us, they signify everything." She pointed to the maguey cactus figures embroidered on the fabric. "It is where we grew up, seeing these plants and the hills. Therefore, your wearing of it is not the same. We only ask for recognition, not robbery. It is the same with our music. It is deep inside us."

I think everyone dreams of a better place than where they are now, wrestling with their problems. Some people can travel for pleasure. Others travel for work. Some kind of dream sustains them. For me, it was pursuit of knowledge, the notion that I could know Mexico—and, by extension, where I grew up in the Southwest—through its folk art. Time spent browsing markets and shops was like an ongoing conversation, building on itself. My house in Georgia has been described as a "Mexican installation." The direct exchange of my money into the hands of the artists was also satisfying, even if it was little for all their time—a day's worth of work for two inches in the case of backstrap weaving. It did not make the bigger pictures of systemic exploitation, which all but the most privileged are exempt from, go away. But as James Brown said about another art form, music, "It makes it all right when it ain't all right." The beauty of a textile can take my breath away, and the idea that it is alive and signifying in its community gives me hope for a community of my own, however illusionary. *Coleccionista* Juan Sandoval, an El Paso librarian I ran into after the 2006 teachers' strike in Oaxaca, observed, "Everything is art. It's all around us. Someone made the clothes you are wearing. Without art, why live?"

Tourists often say "Old Mexico" when they talk about travel. The flying carpet to the past is made possible by air travel. If tourists had to travel by bus, they would not have the same experience of time travel. Train travel was dreamier than bus travel, but not as dreamy as air travel. Joanne Sterricker described landing in the Valley of Oaxaca, looking down at the green fields, the bowl of mountains, the stone churches, and the grazing animals.

"I burst into tears," she told me.

"What was it?" I asked.

"It was coming home, to my childhood," she said.

Of course, if you are learning a language in its native place, you regress to your childhood again, which is what happened to me. But for tourists, a distant land that is folkloric, pastoral, and economically depressed transports them to their grandparents' time, when the surroundings were more like that. A time when people were friendlier, when things were handmade, when people walked more.

So tourist locations find themselves in the dream business, and if it is a classy dream, then locals can take pride in what they have to sell, as Oaxaca does. Their commercialized version of their history, their heritage tourism, enhances their self-esteem. When Lucero Topete, who owns the language school I bring students to, asked her mother what she had thought about the new road through Oaxaca—the Pan-American Highway in the 1930s—she said, "The road brings men." Not a bad thing when you can only marry within your class and choices are limited. Lupita, my Mexican grandmother, said about the tourists, "They make it cheerful." But neither Lupita nor Elda would visit tourist restaurants.

Sheri Brautigam, purveyor of "living textiles" on Etsy, immersed herself in a Mazahua village in the 1970s and observed the textiles worn by the villagers in their living setting. She became a collector, a retailer, and now a guide to bring shoppers to the textiles. She has thought about the impact of the tourist versus the needed money and the impetus to produce and preserve the textile tradition. The best solution, she believes, is to bring foreign visitors to festivals to see the textiles worn in normal cyclical celebrations and for visitors to buy them there, where local people have assembled them for sale. Visitors are normally welcome at these festivals, and they are expected, so their arrival is not a disruption. Sheri is paid by the visitors as a guide, and so the profit from the sales flows directly to the artists. I made the transition from traveler to guide when I left the railroad and started bringing students to Mexico to learn Spanish. I realized it when I wasn't allowed to pay for my dinner at the Restaurante Don Muchos in Palenque. "Guides eat free," they told me. People always know what you are, even if you don't.

Of course art made for tourists is different from art made for the community. Tourist art tries to make the object relevant to the buyer with styles and objects they can use in their very different cultural settings. This ongoing dialogue can be seen played out in FONART stores, which sell indigenous place mats, toiletry bags, blouses with sleeves, dress-length huipils, pencil skirts with waistbands and zippers, indigenous fabric sneakers, purses, flip-flops, and transformations of rebozos into blouses and dresses. The indigenous article of clothing becomes a sign of its former place in the community. I remember when I commissioned pants made of Guatemalan skirt fabric and indigenous women laughed at them because they were a feminine material made into a masculine garment and then worn by a woman. Of course, these are mass-produced for sale because of demand from foreign places where women have worn pants for a long time. When I started buying tourist objects produced by indigenous artists, my Mexican family did not have this type of thing around. Because these items were Indian, they didn't collect them or use them. They had Catholic imagery and objects and a few cheap alebrijes. When they gave me a gift, it was the very Spanish-looking old men made out of corn husks.

As to authenticity and art, the academics are full of caveats. My desire was created by tourism marketing by the Mexican government or, when I was younger, by Fred Harvey and the Santa Fe Railroad publicity department. The artists were enacting their own culture for the benefit of onlookers, who were compensating for something missing in their own societies (Dean MacCannell), or perhaps for the guilt of genocide against the very artists they sought artifacts from (Roxanne Dunbar-Ortiz). So much is wrong with everything I do. But the question remains: What are indigenous people going to do to earn money where they live?

Meanwhile, Mexican women are rapidly adopting couture jeans. Designer blue jeans are made in Mexican maquiladoras. Indigenous men, crossing the border to work in the United States, return wearing jeans. For men, there is now a mix of backstrap-woven pants and jeans. Women still wear complete indigenous dress, but with cotton underpants and turtlenecks. But one of the markers—like speaking Spanish—for indigenous women crossing over into mestizo culture is wearing jeans. Some indigenous women in the city are wearing their traditional huipils with jeans. When I wore jeans in southern Mexico in 1991, I was addressed as "Señor," to call my attention to the fact I was cross-dressing in their culture. Not so anymore. This would still happen with shorts, but jeans now are OK.

I saw a video in which a Guatemalan indigenous woman spoke about poverty, clothing, and her life. She couldn't keep from crying when talking about the poverty. I thought about Rigoberta Menchú's story about what a woman is told about adult life: "that you will have dreams and you will not be able to realize them." I also thought about the anthropologist Walter (Chip) Morris's explication of Maya textile designs, how the wearer puts her head through the center hole of the huipil and completes a circuit, bringing the designs to life, and how personal to the weaver and wearer they are. The designs announce who she is, her status, her family, her community, her protective saints, and her world view.

In Guatemala, indigenous clothing has a blood-soaked recent history. The first thing a visitor notices is that clothing styles, including colors and designs, identify which town an indigenous person is from. Over the centuries, these pueblo designs and colors became codified, highly important to the culture, and perpetuated by the weavers and wearers. During the civil war in Guatemala that lasted from the 1960s to the '90s, indigenous clothing from certain areas marked the wearers as targets. Jean-Marie Simon's photographic record of the war by the army on the peasant villages shows soldiers being trained to recognize indigenous people by their traditional dress. In spite of this, women persisted in wearing their *traje*, or traditional dress, out of pride and resistance. Others, of course, disguised themselves by wearing western dress or by wearing traje from distant villages. It is this historical conversation that bleeds into the fashion touristic exchange. How easy to put on a Nebaj huipil now, when you can admire it as traditional art, when its price will not be a literal eye out of the head, an *ojo de la cara*, my Mexican grandmother Lupita's expression for "expensive."

The specificity of the designs, colors, and techniques to each community in Chiapas and their loss and revival has been explicated in Walter Morris and Carol Karasik's *Maya Threads: A Woven History of Chiapas*. When communities lost their weaving traditions, they could turn to the clothing woven for the saints in the Catholic churches. As Morris points out, it was a happy coincidence that both the Maya and the Catholic Church used textiles for saints' outfits. What was given to the church became a gift back to the weavers. Roads also provided a means of textile-design interchange, and weaving conversations grew up between villages.

It is the complexity of these observed but not understood conversations that gives the cultural tourist such a subtle and attractive spectacle.

"What is tradition?" Carol Karasik said to me. We were talking about the time put into weaving and the new embroideries, which took even more time than the old ones, from Santa Marta, Chiapas. Carol said that a lot of the women who still held to their dress, who were not going to emigrate anywhere, were advancing with education and jobs and were rejecting marriage.

"That's not traditional," I said. I thought about it later.

Tradition is something intrinsic. It's not for sale in any way. It is in the stories that have meaning to a culture, the roots that the people choose to nourish, the new interpretations or actions, in the case of choosing not to marry, that they give to old stories. FOMMA, the Maya women's theater group, has as its mission statement: "We support traditional culture, except those traditions that are harmful to women."

In Zinacantán, Carol told me, tourists didn't know they were purchasing last season's collection. The weavers sought to recuperate thread costs by selling the old $100 blouses for $10 so they could make the new ones. The embroidery was machine made, so it was possible to turn over fashion quickly. The new blouses and skirts incorporated palette changes and were accompanied by accessories, the right color cardigan, the right plastic shoes, and the right handbag. Other Maya in surrounding villages and as far as Lake Atitlan, Guatemala, were buying last season's Zinacantán skirts, as well. At an outdoor bazaar in Coyoacán in 2015, I saw shoes and bags from León that also incorporated material from Zinacantán. The weaving scene is dynamic and alive. This year at the festival of San Lorenzo, a particularly well-dressed woman was wearing a skirt that caught my eye. Its hem was scalloped and embroidered, with contrasting roses embroidered on the upper part of the skirt. Her wedge heels drew the eye to the skirt, and she wore her cape at an angle to the bias designs, the cape in wide panels of pink and purple. The whole ensemble was set off by her salmon cardigan sweater and, the perfect accessory, her pink-and-purple plastic jail-made market basket.

Imagine a whole town in a little valley in the green mountains filled with people dressed like this. Such was my first vision of a Maya town in 1991, and it holds the key to the meaning of the textiles. Eric Chávez Santiago remarked on the same thing in Oaxaca. "In Juchitán and Tehuantepec," he said, "you need a new outfit every year for the festivals. Also, in the Trique area, they use a different embroidered letter every year on the huipil, and you are not respected if you do not weave a new huipil every year."

When traditional clothing is sold as art, it is usually to national buyers. There is a boom in the use of indigenous textiles in fashion in Mexico. Wealthy buyers from Mexico City will wear high-quality huipils on fancy occasions. Mexicans from the Distrito Federal also appreciate references to textile traditions in high-fashion garments. In Oaxaca the crossover from indigenous designs into fashion items has been going on for a long time, with designers making bustiers, purses, and shoes from the traditional isthmus clothing. After the Mexican Revolution a tradition of *indigenismo* arose in Mexican culture, the recognition and appreciation, in principle, of the *mestizaje*, mixed race, of the nation and its indigenous roots. This does not play out in practice, but it does in art. On the International Day of the World's Indigenous Peoples in 2014, the president of the Republic appeared in full Chamulan dress at a celebration in Chamula, Chiapas.

In Mexico City I went to the Shops at Downtown on Isabel la Católica Street. Carla Fernández had a store there, along with

Pineda Covalin and Remigio. Pineda Covalin was among the first to use indigenous designs on silk scarves, ties, and purses. The design was the only reference. The use was entirely modern, and, as the Tlahuitoltepec response to Isabel Marant from the textile museum noted, it "strips identity from the work." In Remigio's store, called Remigio, I romanced a Huave textile with Mazahua embroidery for $600. The garment retained its function as huipil, but it enforced a conversation between the two cultures, recognized only by those who have studied these things. Carla Fernández, in spite of having a traditional Xochistlahuaca huipil—but in a nontraditional silver gray—on her rack, used fragments of indigenous textiles on heavily designed garments with drop crotches, tied leggings, slashed sleeves, and geometrically rearranged capes. Fernández was self-consciously working in the middle ground, crediting her textile producers and their traditional cultures. Other stores in the Shops were also in the indigenous-reference mode: MONGO, which concentrated on home furnishings, and Fábrica Social, which used traditional textiles as the basis for "contemporary design" clothing.

At a bazaar in Coyoacán, my friend Betty and I saw the use of indigenous textiles in fashion items from most of the sellers: Wixárika boots and shoes from the Colectivo Wixari; Nogga, which used rebozo textiles on ballet flats; a León-based boots and purses seller; and a seller of earrings and pendants in resin with Otomí, Mazahua, and Oaxacan textile designs. I would say there is now a boom in the use of indigenous references in modern Mexican fashion, but then, Amusgo and Mixe weavers have been producing huipils for the ruling elite in Tenochtitlán (now Mexico City) since the time of the codices, when they wove them as tribute. "A lot of the Mixe communities make gauze," Eric Chávez Santiago said, "because that was their tribute to Tenochtitlán, which is why their weaving is still so subtle."

Me, I am happy to buy last season's Zinacantecan fashion, as well as the bags from El Camino de los Altos, a cooperative of French designers and Chenalhó weavers, in colors that appeal to me. When I went to Aguacatenango in 2016 women rushed to sell us tourist blouses, but they took them out of jail-made plastic woven carrying bags from the market in San Cristóbal, just like the one I was carrying. I was glad I was on the pulse. I see the vibrant fashion conversation as a result of the proximity of villages to San Cristóbal and a reversal in demographics. San Cristóbal is becoming an indigenous-majority town, but one that has lived with European and North American tourists and academics for a very long time, so that the conversations are all well-known. As Kiki Suárez, the Chiapas artist and textile designer, said when I ran all the complications of this discussion past her, "Everybody borrows from everybody in the fashion business. Smoke a joint. Have a glass of wine."

Shopping is a dynamic encounter. Those who stay at home must have cash from somewhere, and the traveler, the tourist, must have souvenirs. Migration and tourism create intersecting voyages, each participant coming home with something from the other. Retirees move to Mexico to live affordably, and Mexicans move to the United States to earn a living and then, sometimes, return.

One time, on a plane flight to Oaxaca, I sat next to a young Mexican man with his arm in a cast. He was returning home to visit, since he could not work construction in California until his arm healed. We spoke. I had just moved to Georgia, having failed to find a teaching job in California or to buy a house in Santa Cruz. He had bought a house in Santa Rosa, California, as an undocumented worker, filled it with other workers, and was paying it off. It had doubled in value since he had bought it. I felt envy and admiration. I had worked like that on the railroad, but thrown here and there, I never felt settled—so I could not be rooted enough to buy. He was young and fearless and beautiful. "Good for him," I thought. "Brave new world."

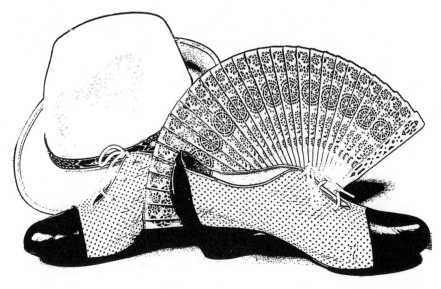

Bandolino Shoes, Fedora Hat, Wooden Fan, Mexico City, 2014. Author's danzón accoutrements.

Danzón

Oaxaca City, February 1992

ONE EVENING, WHEN I was first learning Spanish in Oaxaca, I went to the zocalo to watch the people and eat popcorn for dinner. I had just awakened from my nap and was enjoying what my friend Jim Breedlove, the retired book buyer, called the joy of Mexico—"seeing Mexicans all around." The zocalo was a dance of life and death. Old and young, selling and sex, music and food, protest and celebration, all mixed together.

I was hit on by a teenager asking if I wanted a houseboy, meaning sex.

"*¿Qué?*" I said, although I understood him the first time. "*¿Qué quieres?*" What do you want?

He got my drift and moved away.

"*¿Peines, separadores?*" The Zapotec vendor from the sierra had her straw basket of wooden combs and bookmarks in front of my face. I shook my finger no. The fragrant-gardenia woman was next, and then the rebozo woman, and the child selling chicle gum, but I wasn't in the mood to shop. I was on a mission tonight, to see the Mexican movie *Danzón*, directed by María Novaro, which had just come out. María Rojo played Julia, the telephone operator in the Distrito Federal whose passion was danzón.

The pace of the film was slow, allowing subtleties to build up, without resolution. The smallest detail was the world in a grain of sand.

"Ay, Flaca," Julia's *comadre* at the phone company and at the danzón salons calls her—Thin One. The affection in her friend's voice shows us how much Julia's beauty is appreciated by those around her, even if she does not recognize it herself. At home, being a single mother, she trades critical glances with her teenage daughter. The dancing salon is the only place Julia can let her beauty breathe.

Why danzón, in particular? Why not some other dance?

Danzón is a blend of French country dance, with its quadrangle shapes and called-out steps, which arrived in eastern Cuba with refugees from the Haitian revolution, and rhythms from Africa—a Creole dance. It crossed into Mexico in the 1920s and became the essence of *mexicanidad*, or Mexican-ness. Now, from Mexico, it is crossing back into Cuba for a revival. Elegant, formal, nostalgic, and requiring certain dress codes, the dance recalls a golden age of film and music.

In danzón the musical tension is completed by the dancers, pushing against the constraints of the form, pushing against boundaries, the tiny steps of the female dancer, the rigid upper body, the concentration in the hips of all movement. And the high-heeled shoes.

Julia lives to dance. She and her fellow workers go to the dance salons for romance with married men or, in Julia's case, to compete in contests with her longtime dance partner, Carmelo, who is not her lover. Then the filmic danzón begins its second movement. Carmelo disappears. Julia decides to seek him out, visiting the salons in the city and then taking the train to Veracruz, where he is from. Once she gets on the train, she enters a dreamtime, trains, after all, being machines that transform space into time. This train is more than just a train, and when Julia disembarks in the humid breeze of Veracruz, she is instantly the object of desire of everyone, from the station porter to the drunken Russian sailor in a café on the zocalo. The music of the place then emerges, with Toña la Negra singing a bolero by Agustín Lara as Julia checks into a bordello hotel and befriends a transvestite singer.

"Are you an artist?" she asks.

He paints her lips and gives her costume advice. The climactic scene is her walking in her red dress on the waterfront, seeking Carmelo but finding another, Rubén, a young tugboat captain whose boat is named *Me ves y sufres*, or See Me and Suffer. All the ships have sexualized names, such as the Greek tanker called *Papanikolaou*, after the person who invented the Pap smear test. Rubén, a young man the age of her daughter, does not dance, but with his long hair and his hammock swaying in the night breeze aboard his moored tugboat, he is a more believable *homme fatal* than Tadzio in Luchino Visconti's *Death in Venice*, which this movie reminds me of. If you ask a woman to picture sex, it will most likely be her waking alongside a sleeping lover, savoring the moment, light entering the window. Director María Novaro gives us this scene: Rubén's naked body draped by a sheet, the overhead fan moving it along with the humid air, Julia looking at him, deciding to leave Veracruz because a moment could not be more perfect than this one. You can practically smell the scent of the sea in the room.

The third movement of the danzón is her return to Distrito Federal, with mementos and gifts that suggest, but do not proclaim, her transformation.

Her comadre knows, however, from the subtle touch of her present, a silk scarf, what has happened.

"Ay, Flaca," she says again, meaning it differently this time.

Of course, at the salon later that night, Carmelo reappears, only this time Julia looks him in the eye, a subtle transgression of the rules of the dance.

"Finally," I thought, "sex from a woman's point of view." As María Novaro has said, "The camera is the eye, and the eye is the heart." After seeing this movie, I had to learn to dance danzón.

In June 1995, when I was visiting Guadalajara, I saw a poster in the plaza for dance lessons and a table with two people recruiting. Yes, they could teach me danzón. Yes, today was fine—just pay and get a ticket. With their directions I found an upstairs studio with what looked like an aerobics class full of short teenagers wearing sneakers and sweats. They were jumping around in front of wall-to-wall mirrors as one harried instructor shouting out commands.

"Danzón lessons?" I said, showing her the ticket. What goes on in the minds of bosses?

But I had paid for danzón lessons, and I would get them. She put me in front of the class, where I appeared twice as large as the teenage aerobicizers and awkward in my street clothes.

"Así," she said, demonstrating a move strangely at odds with the music.

"OK," I said, trying to copy her.

The teenagers hopped to their right. She left me to repeat my move and stepped over to issue commands to the exercisers. Back to me, another move side to side.

"Yes." I lumbered along.

Back to the teenagers. Back to me. After fifteen minutes of embarrassment, I attempted to leave, but no dice. There would be repercussions for her. I was here for my hour. When you pay in Mexico, you get your money's worth. No matter what.

Later that year, in November, when I visited Veracruz with my friend Martie, I saw the dance in the square.

When I began taking students to Mexico in 2003, I started to study danzón in Oaxaca, which had a large community since it borders Veracruz. Laura Hernández had a small studio with a wooden dance floor, and her husband was a *jarocho*, a man from Veracruz. She taught me the basic moves and the character of the dance, its many parts and variations. Her Mexican students were teenagers, and they were curious to see an American learning what they thought of as their parents' or grandparents' dance. I always brought my ballroom dance shoes in a little bag and respectfully put them on before I got on her floor.

One has to listen to danzón carefully, since the end of a section, the *remate*, is marked by a lessening of the eleven steps to ten. And it happens abruptly. Then the music reassembles itself with another introduction, and another section starts, with a different tempo. The modern dances of salsa, cha-cha-cha, and mambo evolved from the up-tempo and improvised third section of danzón. As in most Latin dances, from the waist up the dancers don't move, staying in ballroom position. As my teacher Tom Baity in Atlanta put it, "Upstairs in the hotel, everybody is asleep, but in the basement there's a party going on." In danzón the party begins with the last, fast section, called the *montuno*.

Every Wednesday afternoon dancers gathered in the zocalo for danzón with the Marimba del Estado de Oaxaca. As in Veracruz, the dancers claimed the chairs in the front row, came wearing their dresses and fancy shoes, and danced for two hours. There is a saying, *El que canta y baila, la pena se muere.* Who sings and dances, his sorrow dies.

I should mention that dancing is flying. Just as air supports birds' wings, music supports the dancer. Looking out over the garage roof, at the age of ten, at the compost heap below, soft and deep, holding an umbrella. We all have these ideas. No machine necessary. Just poised with a partner on the balls of your feet, waiting for a thermal, waiting for the downbeat. In Atlanta, the jazz club at the Queen of Sheba Ethiopian Restaurant was populated by musicians and singers waiting their turn. And us, discreetly lacing our dance shoes. A nice old wood floor, with only a few traps. The music, thanks to the voyages of the drum, danceable to rumba, son, and foxtrot. Thanks to Tommy Baity's left-hand turn right-hand turn parsing out of the dance floor into angles, we could dance around the tables, easily down an entranceway and back. Bless Tommy, giving the gift of flight. The dance completes the music, with any music from the drum. Resolves the tension in motion. Flying with another person as one. As Tommy says, "Dance like a unit, not a eunuch."

The next year I studied with Laura again, finding her new studio and tracking her down at the cultural center, where she was giving children's classes. I talked my friend Jim into dancing with me, although it was a struggle for him without dance training. I forget how the basic moves of leading another person forward, backward, and in turns seem impossible at first. You need to section the room off into angles and return to the proper angle after a turn.

After the students went home, I spent some time in Mexico City. There was a danzón festival in the Museum of the City of Mexico on Pino Suárez in the historical center. Danzón groups from other states, as well as from the Distrito Federal, were performing. They all had matching costumes, and their friends and relatives were in the crowd. The pastels were like an artificial flower show. Women were in organza and tulle prom dresses with dyed-to-match shoes, but the men's complete outfit included matching short-brimmed panama hats with feathers, two-tone shoes, guayaberas, and matching pants. These were short people, for the most part. And they were dark, but very mestizo as opposed to Indian. There was nothing Indian about this performance, but of course, Africa was submerged in it. How African the dance is has been a subject of controversy in both Cuba and Mexico throughout its history.

I was in Oaxaca again in December 2008, but my teacher, Laura, had disappeared, and I had to find another. The Night of the Radishes, a folk art carving contest featuring radish art, was the following week, and a danzón school belonging to Lulú and Hugo Sosa was offering an intensive five-day workshop. It was here I got a feel for the parts of the dance and the different figures that are performed in each. At this point I had been dancing it for five years and probably had not yet danced one step correctly. Danzón steps are slightly behind the beat, and the tension is created by ending each step or each part on the beat. In that it is like tango. Rushing ruins the character of the dance. While you are learning the mechanics of the steps, it is impossible to be in sync with the music, since you are robotically trying to produce the steps. And there are hundreds of steps—so each danzón is choreographed with the music. Couples prepare for their performances in their danzón organizations with combinations that match each song. In general, the steps are very, very little. *Chiquititos*. So little you cannot imagine. Any large step puts you behind the music. At the intensive, I was still taking steps that were much too large—so I was not yet dancing danzón.

The summer of 2012, I signed up for a month of dancing with Hugo and Lulú's school. The teacher, Lucio, was preparing the group for a festival in two months, so they were learning the choreography for a sequence of eleven steps. Lucio wrote them on the blackboard. We danced in the back of a storefront in a roofed patio on a concrete floor. One day it rained so hard we had to hug the walls and wait while a waterfall from the roof took over the dance floor. Most of the dancers were just struggling to learn the steps. Lucio was always correcting us, but we could not learn why.

One day, late in the month, Lulú dropped by our practice session. "I will demonstrate the steps you are learning," she said.

Lucio instantly transformed from a mule to a racehorse. Lulú lit him up from the first touch. He was now tall and elegant, *el güero*, Fred Astaire. Lulú was curvaceous, and the almost brush of her breasts as she made the flower-tiny turns under the arbor of Lucio's frame was like sex in the mind of God. While we had made stumbling quadrangles, in her movements these evolved into sensuous figure eights, one figure flowing into the next in a dream of the music, slightly behind the beat to create tension, but coming to rest exactly on the point.

We sat transfixed. The danzón was over. Lulú wrapped her magic around herself and bowed out. We applauded. But then we thought, "Never will that happen for me." Later, there was a birthday party danzón for Lulú at the hacienda restaurant in Etla that is used for danzón parties. I was too shy to go to it.

The following summer I finally danced the steps properly. Hugo and Lulú had moved their studio, and Lucio was giving the lessons. We met two times a week for private lessons. The angles, the length of step, where to be in the count on the circle, spins, form. He demonstrated the basic quadrangle, the way the *zocaleros* do it, with too-big steps. Then he danced it with the proper energy.

"*¿Visteis la diferencia?*" Did you see the difference?

The zocalo group was having its yearly five-day festival. Instead of the lesson, Lucio suggested we meet at the zocalo. The final exam. I got there early and saw one of his students, Isabel, in the front row, so she got me a chair. This enabled me to dance with one of the young *danzoneros* from the school in Cuilapan de Guerrero. Another woman who had studied with Hugo and Lulú lent me her husband for a dance, and then her friend, whose husband was not there, asked me to lead. No problem. Finally, Lucio showed up with his dancing partner and after a few dances asked me, and then Isabel, to dance. Of course I missed the lead into the *elegante*, a particularly complex step, twice. But all in all, I followed the other moves. I was dancing in the zocalo.

I still was hesitant about going to their ball, however. The problem: no partner. I asked Jim to come along, but he turned me down. "Go on a Saturday night? Feel like the loneliest man on the planet who ever lived?"

"OK," I thought, "but you would actually be there with someone—but fine."

I had even bought a dress that could possibly be worn at a ball if I should happen ever to go to one.

The day before the ball, I walked into the office at the hotel, and there was a poster up. Ray, the desk man, pointed it out.

"Danzón," he said. He knew I was taking lessons.

"Yes, but no partner," I said.

"Yo," he said. Me.

But he said it in front of the other staff members, who were joking, and so I had to make a joke of it also. And there was Javier, the owner, who would probably disapprove, and Ray, who was probably married, and I always stay at the hotel, et cetera, et cetera. A reminder that I was not really integrated into Oaxaca, coming here on my month-long visits.

The last week in class, Lucio showed me how to break the rules. How the dance is really improvised, within the structure of the steps. He brought in another lead, and I was able to follow him, in spite of the fact that we had never danced together.

"So you can improvise," I said. "And get out of the square."

"Yes," he said, referring to the way some dancers stayed within the rigid box shape. "That's why the dancing in the zocalo is so ugly."

In December I was in Oaxaca for a week to go with Pedro, our guide for the summer students, to Quiotepec, to check it out. One afternoon I paused in the zocalo to watch the danzón. With all the visitors in town, the dancers were even more insular, all wearing their agreed-upon color to separate themselves from any outsiders wishing to dance. Perhaps because I had just arrived and would not stay long, I felt the pushback acutely. I saw how tawdry the outfits were, how unlovely the people, how rigid the steps, how the group defined itself against others. A different perspective from my original one, equally true.

I came back in June for another month of private lessons with Lucio, three nights a week. He gave me three or four new steps in each class, insisted on the form, and occasionally said, "*Bien*." Although I was tired when I arrived at my lessons, the concentration always woke me up. The zocalo group was having their festival again, but I stopped by only a few times. Once I was with my friend Lizbeth, the poet, who felt the group was too exclusive.

"They act like they own the chairs," she said. "They belong to the government. The dancers are retired teachers, and they are self-important."

Lizbeth had issues with the teaching profession, as she worked as a teacher in Villa Alta, a very poor community, and couldn't get a better job. She told me the jobs were for sale. We danced together for a few danzones, causing not a few hostile stares. I didn't know if it was because I was a gringa leading, we were two women, I knew the steps, or Lizbeth didn't. Who knows? A few women in ball gowns and makeup were giving me the look. "Fuck 'em if they can't take a joke," I thought.

I again chickened out on the ball, but before I left I got the lowdown on danzón in the capital from Hugo. He made me out a list covering every day I would be in Mexico City.

"Wednesday is Salón La Maraka in Colonia Narvarte, starting at 3:00 p.m. Thursday is El Gran Salón near Metro Cuauhtémoc, starting at 3:00 p.m. Friday, the California Dancing Club, and Saturday, the Cuidadela at 1:00 p.m." Lucio was pleased. He made me dance all the steps on my own so I could advance next year.

"*¡Que practiques!*" he said. Make sure you practice!

So it was Thursday in Mexico City and a friend, Elena, had come for five days of vacation. We set out for El Gran Salón in a taxi, but the driver left us at the wrong address, so I grabbed a street cab for the remaining five blocks. It was 3:00 p.m. The doors were open, but only so we could get in line for when the doors opened at the official entrance at 4:00 p.m. The huge ballroom, which in a former life was a parking garage, had rows of folding chairs. Danzón dancers carried their shoes and what looked like provisions in bags. They sat in the chairs. We sat also. Next to us was Eduardo, who was wearing white dancing shoes and a maroon guayabera. We talked danzón. This proved to be a fortuitous meeting, since he studied and was a serious dancer. The chairs kept filling up. At 3:45 p.m. everyone rose and made a line outside around the block. Vendors worked the crowd, selling umbrellas and breath mints. They knew their people. Most of the dancers were over fifty, some of the "third age," as they say in Mexico. We were the only foreigners. We finally reached the door, where bouncers were frisking every male and examining the purses of every female. They wore black suits and were huge.

"Are they Mafia?" Elena asked.

"Hopefully," I said. "Then nobody will mess with them."

Eduardo told us to put everything in the well-used checkroom for coats and purses. He guided us to a table near one of the main dance floors. Each dance floor would have five bands, playing until 11:00 p.m. There was no hustle to buy anything, and the admission was only ten pesos, about seventy-five cents. It was as though we entered a portal to another, subterranean world, a fantastic city underneath the everyday one. Eduardo pointed out the great dancers, including one he called El Maestro, who was wearing a hat, a white suit, black shirt and tie, and the same white-and-black, two-tone dancing shoes I had just bought from the Bandolino store across from our hotel, identical except in gender. I was wearing the black skirt I had carried with me in case I needed to go to a ball. And here I was.

Eduardo said something to El Maestro, and he asked me to dance a salsa. Great leads are all the same. They are always a little ahead of you and never repeat themselves. They keep you on your toes. I followed everything, but then I missed the lead for the swivels and then missed it again. I usually miss the lead for the swivels. I had to laugh, and I noticed El Maestro was smiling as well. Life was good.

"She can dance," Eduardo told Elena.

When the danzón band took the stage, Eduardo asked me to dance. They started with "Teléfono a larga distancia," a song that recurred often in the movie. All the dancers faced the bandstand, waiting for the seventh beat to face their partners. We were in dance position, and the first melody began. Eduardo led a square, and then a column, then a lateral, and then a stairway. We were with the music. The month with Lucio paid off. It is hard to use words to describe something that has its joy in the absence of words. The roomful of dancers was one with the music, loved, known, and remembered. Its melody was our words. We achieved the remate, the foreshortened ending, of the first part. Everyone took a break and faced the bandstand again. On the count of seven we began the second part. Now we could dance the flowers, or open moves. Eduardo led a circle in front with a spin on the last three steps. Then the elegante, which you have to know or you will miss. It plays with the rhythm; one holds certain beats, touches toe to floor on others. Then he led a gravevine step, called *menesis*, then a *viloria*, or back *ocho*. We both were feeling the pull to lose ourselves in the music, and Eduardo almost missed the second remate.

"*Danzón tiene muchas trampas,*" Eduardo said. Danzón has many traps.

The third section began with the very familiar trumpet melody, the danzoneros' call to prayer. This was the long-distance call, the lead trumpet playing the melody and the muted trumpet answering in a minor key. African call and response. The rhythm picked up, and Eduardo led the inside flowers, turns by the follower so small that she makes little rose petals with her feet, combined with what is called *alegría*, or happiness, when the leader turns also and the partners are parallel, side by side. Alegría is also the name of a sweet sold on the street, memorialized in a painting by Frida Kahlo showing two women enjoying themselves on an alegría instead of a bed. Where did my mind go? Back to the dance. The reward of a follower is that your mind can drift. A little. Suddenly we were in another remate, *a los dos*, coming out of the alegría.

The fourth section began, really fast now. A time for musical improvisation in the Cuban ancestral dance. Here you can live a little. We firmed up the frame of our bodies and had some surreptitious enjoyment of the sensuality of the dance. There is a name for this enjoyment: *cachondería*, which in the context of dancing translates as "sexiness." This section is what son and salsa do exclusively. But, unlike dancing son, you can danzón all night long.

We danced for an hour and a half. I danced enough that I started to look forward to sitting down. I finally got enough danzón. It became a normal dance to me. Wow, what a lengthy cruise.

The next band was tropical, and Eduardo took me back to our table and promised to return. The following band would be danzón again, and so on until 11:00 p.m. The room was now full, with people who couldn't find seats having to stand in the middle ramp area. Eduardo had told us to leave a drink and something on our chairs, or people would sit in them. Still, with this many people in the room the atmosphere was very polite. Whole families and groups of people were sitting together, often with food they had brought, some clearly celebrating anniversaries of various kinds. Since Elena was not dancing, we decided to leave, as it was now 6:30 p.m. Eduardo returned just as we were getting up, and I thanked him for the dances.

"*Hasta la próxima,*" he said. Until the next time.

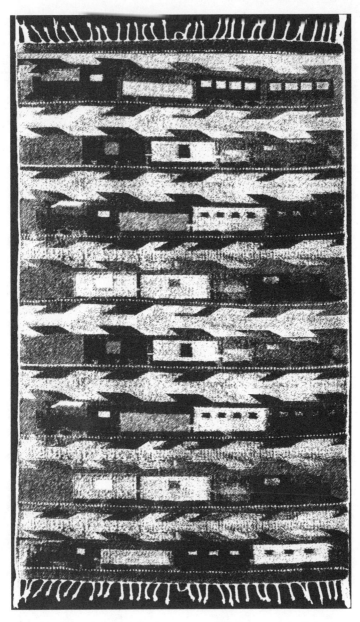

Train Rug, Teotitlán del Valle, Oaxaca, 1994. Wool, 52.4 × 31 in. Private
collection.

Tesmole

Santiago Quiotepec, Oaxaca, Christmas 2013

I READ ON the Internet that 1.6 million Mexicans returned home for Christmas, and the *federales* escorted them south from the US border in caravans to prevent incidents.

Our longstanding guide Pedro's daughter was going for a PhD in philosophy, so when Pedro and I went to Santiago Quiotepec at Christmas to scout a field trip location for the students, we spent the drive discussing Plotinus. Not that I know anything about Plotinus, but it was a starting point for talking about God. Neither of us believed in God, but we had both spent a lot of time thinking about it. Pedro was relieved to find another like himself. Pedro had been telling me about the La Cañada region in Oaxaca for years now because he had taken a cactus specialist there. It had an old railroad depot, recently abandoned by dwindling passenger service, and we thought of writing a book together, about similar places where old railroaders might still live. I could talk to them about "the company," and Pedro could write about the culture, how specific it was to each little place. Santiago Quiotepec, for example, grew *huacle* chiles, and the next town over controlled a canyon where military macaws still lived in the wild.

"These towns were inaccessible by road for many years," he told me, "and the railroad was the only way to get goods out, like huacles and macaw feathers."

I thought about it. I associated the railroad with mining and heavy freight. The thought of boxcars full of feathers amused me. It seemed surreal. I remembered the church in Chiapa del Corzo with a wrought iron bedstead in it, covered with a netted and embroidered bedspread. It was inside the church to show off the embroidery.

We followed Highway 135, only built in the 1970s. There were many railroad stations, now abandoned, along the route that climbed northwest over the ranges sitting below the Sierra Madre Oriental to the east. As we came out on the northern slope, a broad river lay below us, running large even during the dry season. Organ cacti looking like upright hands covered the desert ranges. Green cottonwoods followed the river, as did the defunct rails. Because of the rare cacti and the macaws, La Cañada was part of a biosphere now that included parts of Puebla as well. In the Late Classic period the area was under the control of Monte Albán and was on the trade routes to the Pacific Coast and up into central Mexico. The area had excavated and unexcavated archaeological sites. Santiago Quiotepec had one overlooking the modern village. We had lunch in Cuicatlán on the way, and Pedro and I ate fish after he told me they came from lakes and not the far-off coast. The restaurant overlooked the abandoned train station on the riverside. Entrepreneurs had begun to pull the rails out, and they hung like iron noodles on the riverbanks. The railroader in me had an envy attack. I could imagine the river run down from Tehuacán through the canyons on the iron road. You would never get tired of this red-bluff, sere-green desert mood.

On our way again, we had to stop because a community group was holding the road hostage, so we paid the fifty pesos to pass.

"This is not really the solution," Pedro said. The mayor had spent the New Year's distribution money, given by the state government for public works, and the community felt ripped off. "So they rip us off."

Nothing new, in my experience. Just another missing receipt form for the university's accountants to ponder. We were going to take the students to Santiago Quiotepec in the summer if the new tourist cabins the villagers had built were comfortable. The turn-off was just past the macaw reserve in Sabino Canyon. To see the birds you used to have to spend the night in primitive cabins and before dawn climb to the rim.

"You had to be fast," Pedro said. "If you were not a professional photographer, all you saw was a whoosh of green, and you thought, 'Did I just get up and climb for an hour for this?' There was no electricity in the cabins. They gave you flashlights, but you were wondering what was in there with you."

Santiago Quiotepec had completed its road since the last time Pedro was there, and it was no longer necessary to drive across the railroad bridge on the wooden beams the rails had rested on. We walked over it anyway, and you could see villagers wading across the river to reach their goat herds on the other side. An ancient aqueduct hugged the bluffs next to the river. The community radio was playing on loudspeakers everyone in the valley could hear.

Pedro had visited most of these villages in his role as a teachers' union representative. "That's life in these communities," Pedro told me, referring to the radio announcements. "So-and-So is making tamales—there is some meeting—and they wake you up for church at 6:00 a.m."

"Could have its downside," I thought as the cumbia music enforced itself on our consciousness.

The new tourist cabins had hot water, electricity, bunk beds, and windows that shut out the steady wind gusts that blew down the valley in the afternoon. They could sleep sixteen, they had their own kitchens, and the facility offered access to ten bicycles and a dozen horses. You could take guided excursions to the ruins to see the rosetta cacti that grew on the canyon walls, or you could ride through the abandoned railroad tunnels. The cook was away, so we were directed to a private home for dinner. We sat at their outside table with the grandmother while the cook fixed us all *tesmole*, the local specialty stew.

"The base for all these moles is corn," Pedro told me. "Then the local huacles give their distinctive flavor."

He had guided gourmet groups for Susana Trilling, who had a cooking school in Oaxaca City. Up the highway toward Tehuacán, another village produced salt, and the local dish was roasted maguey worms. Santiago Quiotepec had a small local cactus fruit, *tepesquite*, that each weekend was trucked to the Sonora Market in Mexico City to supply the Quiotepecanos who went there for work and could not be without their valley's tastes. I wondered where they went in the United States and how they got supplied there. The tesmole arrived, in brown glazed dishes, a rich brown stew textured with a red chile and corn base, and containing a huge hunk of ox foot, delicious squash, and corn on the cob. Fresh corn tortillas accompanied it. And for Pedro, a cerveza, a beer.

"*Provecho*," the grandmother wished us. "May it agree with you."

When Pedro and I arrived with the students the following

June, the wind was still blowing through the canyon in the afternoon, but it was hot now and ripening the *chicozapotes* and mangoes. I had seven students, and we would spend two nights in the
tourist cabins. The Atlanta students were all urban, with the
exception of the Nigerian, Precious, and Carlos, who had been in
the army in Afghanistan. We turned off the paved highway onto
a dirt road that dove down to the river, past palms and cacti:
pachyderm, viejitas, *columna trajana*, and *tetechos*. I could see the
orange flash of the railroad bridge that was part of the old road.
Several of the students had inhaled but hadn't exhaled.

At the bottom Pedro parked in front of the railroad bridge, and
we all balanced our way to the middle of the bridge to look at the
river's S curves and hear goats bleating and boom-box *ranchera*
music. The white dome of the church steeple rose above the green
tree line. The town was in two parts. The one where the railroaders lived was near the station, now converted to a bus depot.
Against the far bank across the river, the main part of town centered around the basketball court in the patio of the municipal
offices. Dirt streets and mostly adobe houses and grocery stores
were the rule, but some concrete and rebar buildings were going
up with remittance money from migrants who had gone to the
United States.

"Most of the town is gone," Ana, the hostess at the cabins, told
us. She had a six-month-old baby and no husband. Her sister
cared for the infant while she worked.

That night the students went to the little groceries and bought
beer to drink on my porch. I heard them for a while, but then I
went to sleep, since I knew where they were. In the morning we
went to climb to the pyramids on the mountaintop above Santiago
Quiotepec. In ancient times it was a Mixtec-controlled zone, but
the people spoke Cuicatec. We left early, but still the heat took

over, and Ayanna, who had asthma and forgot to bring her inhaler, had an attack on the climb. All I had was a HALLS cough drop, but the menthol calmed her. Pedro, meanwhile, had left town with his city shoes and had forgotten to bring water—I gave him half of mine—and a hat. He did have a bag of mangoes, however. We climbed for three hours, stopping to eat mangoes at promontories. A camera crew from *Museos sin paredes*, Museums without Walls, an ecological tour organization sponsored by the government, joined us, filming the guide and the students. At last we reached the central plaza, and the students scampered up the steps to see the joining of the two rivers that would eventually reach the Papaloapan River and the Gulf Coast. To the west were the blue mountains of the Mixteca, their rivers draining into the Pacific. It was worth the climb, although I had hesitated in the morning. The students were taking selfies of themselves emerging from the tombs. The way down was considerably easier than the way up, even though it was now full noon and desert hot.

"I kept thinking I just don't have enough on," Carlos told me later. He meant a flak jacket and weapons. He was flashing back to Afghanistan.

Ana took the young women of our group under her wing, particularly the non-swimmers. I knew everyone would want to get in the river, so Ana played with Precious on the sandbanks while Riah, Ayanna, Tanner, Luther, and Opal tried floating the shallow rapids. Nobody took my advice to keep their shoes on, so I was the only one who could stand up. The rest were tumbled downstream and spit into an eddy where an old man had taken his two burros to get a drink. Then a true cowboy picked his way along the bank on horseback. The students were in beachwear, yellow striped suits and bikinis with diaphanous cover-ups.

Suddenly a lot of locals found things to do near the river. None of us realized we were burning like meteorites. But now it was time to climb up the trail to have our lunch of tesmole and a siesta.

At five, we took yet another hike, an hour's descent down the rocky cliffs above the river, to see the rare Echevería cactus, locally called rosetta, in its natural surroundings. The arroyo we descended was moist year round from a spring feeding it, and the acrid fragrances of desert plants and flowers mingled with our sweat and new smells carried on the wind as we rounded corners and balanced on the rocky trail down.

"What goes down must come up," I told Pedro, who was keeping up the pace. His macho side had kicked in, since he had to be as tired as I was. He had produced yet another bag of mangoes.

The three girls who declined the hike went with Ana to the mango grove, where they got to see a boa constrictor who lived in a tree. They became Facebook friends later, and it was them Ana waved to as we left early to go to Teotitlán del Camino to eat worms for breakfast. Luckily, they were out of season, and we ate goat tacos in the meat section of the market instead. On the way back to Oaxaca, we almost ran out of gas, since the Pemex station was inexplicably closed. I told uplifting stories to Pedro to keep his mind off the gas tank. We laughed over the printed sign made up for ecotourism villages: *Actividades: arqueología, bicicletas, cuevas, sentarismo.* Activities: archaeology, bicycles, caves, sitting.

"I think they made a mistake," Pedro said. "It should be *senderismo.*" Hiking, not sitting.

We made it up to the top of the canyon, past the spot where we saw a motorcyclist pushing his out-of-gas bike last December, and found the next Pemex station. Because it was Sunday, they would not take Pedro's credit card. The station convenience store was filled with families dressed for a prom, black suits with ties and long, flowing dresses.

"Protestants," Pedro said. "They have to dress like this."

I remembered my own struggles as a child to wear cowboy boots to church. "God doesn't care if I wear my chaps," I told my parents. It didn't fly. I would never have gone for the prom dress.

When I got back to the hotel I lay down and got up five hours later, regretting the goat taco. I was insect bitten, sunburned, and limping from sore muscles. All the students were back with their homestays. Life was good.

The students composed their own descriptions of the trip: "Somewhere in Mexico, two flights and a three-and-a-half-hour twisty drive into the Cañada region of Oaxaca, is a tiny town called Santiago Quiotepec," wrote Opal Mason.

Among the dust and the cacti, I have climbed back behind our little cement rooms and up the hill with Tanner, Carlos, and Luther. We stand at a lookout point above the small town, and I see the winding river that has worn the mountain down, the yellow bridge, the mountains that go on and on. The evening wind is blowing dust through my curly hair. We look below to see the church building's white dome, the source of the now clanging bell. Fireworks interrupt our quiet thinking, but the sound cannot impede my fantastic view. Walking a little way from the others, my eyes are filled with tears. 'God made it and saw that it was good,' I think to myself, filled with utter joy in awe of the spectacular land before me. I think of Linda's sparse wording regarding our weekend destination as I write in the dusty wind after dinner. She had brought us out here in the wilderness of Mexico to lose ourselves for a weekend. She had brought us out here so that we could find a piece of ourselves that no Atlanta skyline could reflect. In the wild wind and the mountain paths, as we were guided up and down miles of historical secrets, as our bodies sweat and were cooled, I truly felt wild and alive, full of purpose and adventure. I found such joy in the simplicity of living and the peace of nature. In the morning, my fingernails stained yellow with mango juice and with dust in all the creases of my toes, I wake up to the sound of a flute. It takes me two songs to realize that the flute is a record being played over the town's loudspeakers, but the gentle music of Paul Simon on a hot desert morning is a memory that lingers at the edges of my consciousness.

This, from Carlos Thompson, who did two tours in Afghanistan:

The smell of goat shit dusted my nostrils as I squinted my eyes, the blowing sand being shoved into my mouth by the wind. I wanted to see the town from above, and we were excited to get a better view of the valley. Once we approached the cliff's edge, I thought about the beauty of the mountains surrounding Quiotepec. The air felt like a warm blanket around my shoulders and I didn't notice the dust anymore.

In 2007, I had the same feeling on a poorly constructed overwatch, overlooking the Korangal Valley as it loudly wailed and hurried itself away from Camp Keating and into Pakistan. Then I was so nervous I nearly had to remind myself to breathe. When I finally did inhale, I took a long gulp of dipping-tobacco-tainted spit and instantly puked my guts all over the mountain's side. I thought about how the enemy scouts must have been watching and how young and pathetic I looked, pacing around with a gun half my size, sweating through my armor and mumbling prays to God for mercy.

Now it is 8:00 p.m. in Quiotepec, and as the sun shines a dim red across the sky and the church bell roars in the background, the sound of howling fireworks rips in the sky and explodes like missiles in a dogfight movie. I could feel how light my shirt and shorts felt on my body and hugged myself in hopes to find my rifle. I wanted the security of all the armor I wore almost a lifetime ago. The unbearable weight and heat. The anger, the taste of my own vomit and the pain of an empty stomach to make those explosions in the sky make sense. My eyes felt wet when I saw the smoke. I looked back down the path and said almost simultaneously with the other students, 'We are late for dinner. We should head back down.' I was happy for them and felt better that the rings and booms for them were just bells and fireworks. Early 20s is a good time to explore a mountaintop. It's a good time to hear the bells and fireworks and only worry about homework, the next writing prompt, or will my family like the gift I got them from Mexico. I try my best to worry about the same things now, so late in life, and it's very hard. It's good to be around people whose world still matters to them and I have nothing to do with it. My wife is a good woman for making me go to Mexico.

During the war years, many veterans like Carlos came with me to study in Oaxaca. They were using their GI benefits. Mexico reminded them of Iraq or Afghanistan, and they had a hard time switching gears. I remembered the previous summer with a group I had called "the unit" because there were so many ex-soldiers with me and because they went everywhere together. I took them for ice cream on the patio of the Basilica of Our Lady of Solitude, and half the group dropped to the ground when some people set off fireworks in the plaza, something that happens nearly every day there. Little children running up to them would paralyze them. One of the group, Derek Rider, had e-mailed me before the trip and asked me if I thought his homestay family would think he was odd if he stayed in his room and drank every night.

"They would probably like it better if you would invite them to join you," I told him.

The first day in Oaxaca, waiting for school, Derek Rider, who had done three tours in Iraq and earned a Purple Heart, had this experience:

> After a light breakfast, my host mom walks me to the school, which is conveniently located only two blocks away from the home where I am staying. All the way there I am continually analyzing the objects, people, cars, buildings, and noises around me. There is an assortment of cars parked along both sides of the streets. Colorful storefronts and a school make the area feel safe and normal. However, I am on high alert looking down the side streets, looking at doorways, windows, and constantly looking over my shoulder to insure that no one is following me. I arrive at the school safely and the mother leaves me to fend for myself until the large metal gates are opened promptly at 8:30 a.m. It is only 8:15 a.m. when I am left to fend for myself. I immediately place my back against the wall of the school so that there is a hard surface behind me and I can see down both sections of the sidewalk. I hear a tapping noise off to my right. I look over to see a blind man with his cane tapping his way along the sidewalk. I give him a quick glance as he is approaching, adjust my feet to give him plenty of room and continue looking for my friend who is running late. No more than five seconds pass when something collides with the right side of my body and I am startled. I look over instantly to see

the blind man looking directly at my chest. He is using his cane to tap my shins and feet to determine what exactly is in his way. I don't know whether to punch him in the throat and make a run for it or try and move out of the way. Luckily, for the sake of the blind man, a woman comes to his rescue. She takes him gently by the arm, says something in Spanish and points him in the right direction. At no time during this encounter and rescue does the woman ever look at me. As soon as the blind man is on his way the woman scurries across the busy street and continues on her way. I am still standing there wondering what in the hell had just happened to me.

Desireé was a 110-pound Marine, last deployed in Iraq. She became my hero the last weekend of my trip with "the unit," when we were in Puerto Escondido. My strategy with the students was to put them in an environment where they couldn't hurt themselves. So I found an isolated hotel next to a safe swimming beach and ten minutes away from a beginning surfing beach. Being broke at the end of the trip, they happily took the bait. Beach boys were hawking surfing lessons, and I could see Desireé getting interested.

"Could I do that?" she asked.

"Go for it," I said. The waves were about four feet high, and the instructors gave the students a crucial shove so that they could catch them. Day one, Desireé and the other students caught waves and got upright. Day two, they were on their own, and catching waves was harder. About midday, Desireé caught one that put her on the rocks. We all went running up, but she was OK. Just scratched up and scared.

"I thought I was going to drown," she said. But she didn't return the surfboard. In about an hour, she took it back in and chased the waves until sunset. She didn't catch any to ride, since the rocks incident had left her drained of energy, but she tried all afternoon. Later I gave her the camo Band-Aids from my first aid kit.

"Wow, these are cool," she said. "I didn't know they came in camo."

"Camo and Hello Kitty," I said, "but I'm keeping the Hello Kitty."

Lacquer Carousel, Temalacatzingo or Olinalá, Guerrero, 2015. Lacquer on gourd, 12 × 11 in. Private collection.

Sabor, Flavor

Oaxaca City, June, 2015

BARBARA, MY FRIEND who introduced me to Oaxaca, in her last years still came to Oaxaca, and occasionally we were there together. At home in Santa Cruz, she had lost consciousness while driving and hit a dumpster, so things had started to go wrong with her being out in the world on her own. In Oaxaca our mutual friend Lizbeth and I would set up meeting points with her, but she would always go to the zocalo instead, so we finally just looked for her there.

One night we were going to meet at Candela, a club for salsa dancing. Barbara could hardly walk at that point, but she still danced, staying in one spot on the floor, swaying to the music, and enjoying the young men. (Not long before, when Little Joe y La Familia, the Chicano band, had come to Santa Cruz, we had managed a polka.) Anyway, according to her, she told the taxi driver where to take her, and he kept driving around the block and stopping outside Catedral, a restaurant.

"No, no," Barbara said. "Catedral!" He would drive around the block again. She finally realized she wasn't saying, "Candela" and managed to get to the club.

Barbara has always been my mentor in the enjoyment of life.

Kennesaw State University was entrepreneurial, meaning that you could teach whatever you wanted as long as you were willing to do all the work yourself. Because of this, I had been able to incorporate the study of Mexico in all my classes. I was giving myself and my students the kind of education I wished I had had growing up in Southern California, in what used to be Mexico. Even exploring the railroad in American culture came around to Mexican pickers being needed in the West and the connection of the north and south through rail, a connection that is still being utilized by migrants who ride "the beast" all the way from Guatemala to cross the Mexico-US border at Eagle Pass, Texas. Teaching creative nonfiction meant that I could weave the history, memoir, and poetry of the whole hemisphere into our reading list. Then there was the summer opportunity to actually go. Some purely writing students came south with me because of the reading list. Others interested in history or Spanish language discovered writing. Finally being able to settle down and be a scholar has been a fair trade-off for losing the continual motion of the railroad life. Although I still do get an occasional flashback when we head down a vertical dirt road on one of our field trips; I enjoy the rush, particularly since it is not happening at 3:00 a.m.

I think I kept taking students to Mexico to integrate my life, hoping to incubate some Pan-Americanism into the consciousness of Georgia. The difficulties of traveling with them were familiar to me. Having put down the bottle myself, I was disappointed that the students weren't ready to, and I saw how self-centered and complaining the drinking made them. The soldiers I could forgive more easily—they were almost Guatemalan in their psychic fractures. They would probably need alcohol for many years, and better to drink it in Mexico, where people loved them anyway. A lot of Mexicans were drinking away similar nightmares. What I really wanted was to have others see what I saw there, or at least to look. The past few years it seems like more of them have. Maybe I should quit now, while I'm ahead.

Zen gardens have a low gate. You must bow to enter the garden. When I first got to Mexico, I was early for everything, impatient if a store was closed for the day, angry if an ATM was out of service. It would take me a week to be in watery rhythm with the place, the way sleeping beside a river links up your pulse to the water. Mexico was centered. It had, as they say in aikido, weight underside. Mexicans needed to be centered to deal with the constant push of their environment, the expected frustrations that led to the expression "*Si Dios quiere*," If God wills it. They had a counterplan, to warm every encounter with human contact and to wake up every morning with new hope, since every day had a character of its own.

I don't live that way in Georgia or anywhere else in the United States. I am too big, too hurried, and too desperate to fill my needs to get into the Mexican mind-set. Consumer society tells me I should never be thwarted, contradicted, or questioned, and when I am—by traffic, computer glitches, service centers in India, or lines in a restaurant—I am enraged, but I learn nothing because everyone else around me is behaving the same way. In Mexico, they are not.

The second week in Oaxaca, I liked to take the students to the big market, called Abastos. There is one everywhere in Mexico, right next to the second-class bus station. All the students were warned by their Mexican families not to wear jewelry or take too much money. I was warned by an expat that there was a band of five young women who would surround and rob me.

"Five?" I said. "No problem, they're short."

She just looked at me. "Can't be worse than controlling five loaded boxcars with hand brakes," I thought.

On our trip in summer 2015, before we went inside the eight-block-long market, I took them to the second-class bus station across the road. This was not the transportation they were used to. Inside the huge, cavernous roundhouse with competing bus lines, people in leather sandals were carrying large plastic grain bags tied with twine or refrigerator-sized cardboard boxes. The students looked nervously around.

"This is where you go if you are really traveling here," I told them. "You can get anywhere—to a village on top of a mountain—anywhere from here." I saw one student's eyes light up. He would be back. In Georgia you can't get anywhere on the bus.

On the way back, we caught another city bus, and a student said, "Their transportation system really works."

By the way, a student was robbed by five older women in the market closest to the city center. She said, "It was crowded, and the person in front of me stopped, and then I was hemmed in. When I got outside, I saw my wallet was missing from my backpack."

I thought, "Why were you carrying your wallet in your backpack?" I had thought someone had stolen my Versace sunglasses out of my shoulder bag when I was dumb enough to leave it open on the seat beside me in the Mexico City airport while playing "Solamente una vez" on my ukulele. When I got home I found them under my bed.

Most of their excursions are overprotected by me. The trips with Pedro are meant to be slightly more spontaneous, since we go to places unvisited by North American tourists. This is where most of them have their revelations.

The summer of 2015 I didn't plan ahead for our field trip with

Pedro. I knew we had too many people to fit into the cabins at Santiago Quiotepec, so I asked Pedro to take us somewhere new. Of course I knew that unless you are very flexible, you really have to check out the accommodations in advance in person, but once back in the United States, I forgot that. We do everything online instantly, and Mexico has learned to offer things to us this way, but that does not change the reality. I started three months early asking Pedro for the details, but up until a day before we left Georgia, I had no idea where we were going. He had tried to make advance reservations, but the community with the cabins canceled at the last minute. So we were doing it the Mexican way, just going there. Of course, the students expected to know everything they were going to see in advance as well. In particular, Lissa, my student assistant, was a highly organized person, and I could tell Mexico was messing with her head.

I had told them it would be cold the first night and then hot the second. I tried to keep communications short and to the point, since students now do not communicate in spoken language—they text. I should have said, "OMG snow" or something, but I only said, "Cold." Nobody brought sweaters. Well, except me. They had been at the foot of the Sierra Juárez with its huge blue mountains assembling the Gulf rainstorms every afternoon, but they hadn't really thought about it. We were going over them, staying on top the first night in the Chinantec-speaking area. Pedro had been to all these towns, teaching the teachers.

The first crisis was finding the bathrooms in Ixlán de Juárez. After leading a line of students from door to door asking for bathrooms, like little ducks following a roll of toilet paper, we finally found one store with an operating toilet.

"What gives with the water?" I asked.

"Doña, they are cleaning the tanks for the whole town."

"How often do they do this?"

"Twice a year."

How would you know this, of course? The Pemex gas station looked modern, except that twice a year, it wasn't. We went on. I had assembled a barf kit the day before, since one of the students, Jimmy, was down with *E. coli*. He had thrown up three times on the floor of my apartment in Oaxaca City during my writing class. He now had undisputed rights to the front seat in the van. We were in pine forest soon, with bromeliad sloths sleeping in the trees. A road crew was cutting trees, and the smell of cut pine invaded us. Pedro was looking for the cabins after the turnoff for the town that operated them, but we weren't seeing them. He made a U-turn, and we went down the road to Santiago Comaltepec to ask directions—a long way down the dirt road, the steep, hairpinned dirt road, past cornfields, little streams, cattle, donkeys, dogs, and tin-roofed houses. Finally, we were in streets too narrow to turn around in, with the church dome hovering above the lesser roofs, all at a vertical angle to the valley floor thousands of feet below.

"*Disculpe. ¿Cabañas?*" Pedro asked a local farmer.

"*Sí, pero allá.*" Yes, but back up there.

Since we were down here, Pedro decided to look around the town center. The only flat place was a courtyard in front of the old church, dated 1604, and a spectacular blue basketball court with a soft floor, lighting, roof, and bleachers. It kind of stood out. It wasn't the standard government-issue court. I remembered writer Sam Quinones's story about the Oaxacan basketball players in Los Angeles in his book *True Tales from Another Mexico*. There were so many immigrants from the mountains of Oaxaca that they formed their own basketball leagues in California. And so, when we got to meet the mayor of Comaltepec,

I asked if the migrants had contributed to the building of the court.

"Yes," he said. "Many people from here go to work in LA and send money back for basketball."

For me, this made our excursion worthwhile. Georgia also has an immense migration from Mexico and Central America. Here the students were on the other end of it, petting the dogs, eating green apples, and talking to the mayor and municipal workers about the great snow in 2008. No textbook could have given that to them. The only other English-speaking visitors Comaltepec had were from the Summer Institute of Linguistics in Mitla, Oaxaca—evangelicals on a mission. We had no mission—we were just lost.

After chatting up the mayor, we hopped in our vans and took another road back to the highway. It was nearing dusk when we arrived at the cabins, which were attached to a roadside restaurant, on the pass to Valle Nacional and in the warmth of the Gulf. Clouds were surrounding us like the blankets we did not have many of in the cabins. As for the cabins, there were three of them and thirteen of us. There were six beds and some foam cushions and poly blankets. Fireplaces with wet wood. The students would have to double up in the beds, and Pedro and his son Alan, who was driving the other van, would have to take the pads. When we first looked at the accommodations, Pedro offered to take Alan back to another village that might have more cabins, but looking at where we were situated on the road—right on the road—I asked him to stay with us. Who knew who might show up on a road? I pictured the students drinking in the café late into the night. No, I wanted the vans here. Of course, he agreed.

I put off walking around until the morning, preferring to sit happily by the fire. But the students ate and took a hike from which they could see eternity, into their pasts, into their futures. For one of the students, Liz Hutchison, it was a moment of reunion with her departed father's love for Mexico. As she later wrote:

It was truly unlike anything I had ever seen before. From high above the mountain ground, I saw the universe below me. Clouds danced around charcoal mountaintops in varying shades of blue. On top of some of the mountains I could make out distinct outlines of trees that looked like giant mushrooms of clovers from a Dr. Seuss book. It seemed just as incredible and infinite as the gas clusters in Andromeda. This would have been the most golden opportunity I had ever had to take a photo, but I was too scared to lean, with one frozen hand on the ladder, over a plateau on the side of a mountain, only in order to take my phone from my back pocket to snap a photo.

And so I stood in silence, eyes open, heart bursting, and something warm working its way into the center of my gut— nervousness, exhilaration, and communion with the other- worldly. I could feel the souls of the spirits I had imagined living inside the trees and, amongst the ancient Chinantec war- riors and gods, I felt something more familiar, my father's freckled hands in my own, living in that holy moment.

Jimmy Peters also transcended his own problems. "For some reason the crisp air, the cold and the beauty simply made every- thing I was physically feeling disappear," he wrote. "But my feel- ings and thoughts, of what was outside myself and beyond my control, were coming to life. All week, I just wanted to not be sick. I knew just when an episode in the bathroom was coming and just how my body felt at each moment. What I wasn't until that moment, on the mountain's peak looking out on the sunset with classmates, was fully there."

"Looking back, I don't think that the view was necessarily the purpose of our trip," observed Lissa Small. "It was perhaps part of it, but I have since come to believe that the entire experience, good and bad, new and unusual, beautiful and exotic, was the purpose of the trip."

In the morning one of the women noticed a large tarantula on the beam above her bed, fortunately obscured by the dark the night before. I remembered finding them in the desert near El Paso when I worked nights, standing alone a half mile from the caboose, waiting for the engine lights of a passing train. They were big but harmless.

In spite of being cold, jumbled together, lost, and sharing their cabins with scary insects, the students were surprisingly cheerful. Something was different this year. I think it was because nobody was drinking too much. The far side of the mountains sheltered an ecological niche of tropical rain forest, as different from the near side as day from night. Huge tree ferns, bromeliads, waterfalls, and palms flourished under the hot breath of the Gulf Coast. The land was held collectively by the Chinantec pueblos, so development was all on the public road, just little restaurants selling honey and bananas. We had a reservation in some cabins that had a Facebook page, so I had at least seen pictures of them. But we stopped early at a natural swimming hole in the river, surrounded by a park with cabins of its own. Leaving the students there to swim, Pedro, Alan, and I went on to look at the other cabins and to realized the Internet pictures had not conveyed their moldy air. We decided to stay where we were, and we found a grill across the road, for tasty sausages, chicken, ribs, and steak. Two students relaxed in hammocks they had brought from Georgia, and the rest spent the day underwater in the stream that came right out of the ground at its *ojo de agua*, its spring. That night one of the students locked the key to a cabin inside, and we discovered the management left at dusk. I wandered around until I saw a lighted house surrounded by barking dogs, and I shouted out. Indeed, it was the house of the caretaker.

"How did you find me?" she asked, letting us into the locked cabin. Just in time for a roof-rattling thunderstorm that put me right to sleep.

Others had a few insect encounters, a scorpion in the shower, beetles in the mattresses, but with this group I didn't hear about them until the morning. Bless their hearts.

We left in the morning in a rain and fog that let us see about a foot ahead of us on the road until we crested the mountains, where it all stopped. Two weather climates right next to each other. We passed up the smoked trout everywhere on offer in the sierra in order to get back and let the students do their homework for Monday. Still no water in Ixlán de Jaúrez.

The final weekend we flew to Huatulco, on the coast, for a luxurious beach experience, but it was the difficult mountain trip that the students talked about as mind changing.

By living with Mexican families the students get the chance to regress that I had with Lupita and Elda. They have a Mexican mother, they are fed and protected and become more open. Someone is happy when they speak baby Spanish. Then they need a journey in which they meet themselves in a mirror—they need complications they can triumph over or recover from. They can rise up from an illness or find their way home or understand that they have a right to be on the planet.

My writing classes I often think of as a support group,

sometimes an abuse support group or a trauma support group. One year it was a suicide recovery support group. Very often it is a religion recovery group, the students fighting their way out of fundamentalist judgments. When the writer Sam Quinones visited my class one year, he remarked on how many students were writing about religious recovery.

"Nobody believes in God in LA," he said.

Well, they do in Georgia. One of my students, writing about his life, referred to himself as "the son of man." His moment of illumination came when he put a loaded gun beside his head, pulled the trigger, and nothing happened. He knew he needed to change everything.

I am not saying Mexico fixes every problem, but it certainly helped the vets, helped the young women who felt judged every moment of their lives, and it helps me, every year, move an inch out of the center of the circle so that I can see another point of view.

What a relief that is.

I was afraid I would lose the freedom I was accustomed to in Mexico by bringing students, and to an extent that has been true. I couldn't be like Barbara, just dancing in the midst of dementia. But I look at the situation like a passenger train, where the first consideration is the safety of the passengers. I try to provide a safe environment, finding a beach hotel where they can walk to a beach that is safe for swimming, so that when they get drunk at night and think it would be a good idea to swim in the ocean, they won't kill themselves in the surf. This, like working on the railroad, doesn't allow me to take chances personally, since I have to be there for them. But then, I was used to living that way. On the railroad I had to be extra careful in my daily life, because an injury would mean I couldn't work. Mexico originally freed me up from a lot of that anxiety, but now I had to bring enough of it with me to be responsible for the students. It was always a relief to put them on the plane for home. Perhaps that is why I enjoyed bringing my dance teacher Tommy Baity down one year, because that year I got to dance through Mexico.

Tommy came down to Oaxaca the summer of 2003, and I found him a basic rooftop room in the house, now a pensión, where the famous painter Rufino Tamayo was born. I had two friends with me on the trip, Joanne, who was studying Spanish, and Caroline, my girlfriend. Caroline immediately rented a studio and began drawing pastels of what was in the market. Tommy had sciatica from his grueling teaching schedule, and so I told him about Baños Reforma. This was a public bathhouse around the corner, where you could rent cubicles with steam and a round shower head in the ceiling for ice-cold water. Men could get massages from men. My friend Lloyd had already told me that a "complete" massage was also available. It was around $10. Tommy went every day. I missed my chance for a complete massage one time when the little man came to the door of my cubicle offering and I insisted on the rules.

"*Soy mujer*," I am a woman, I told him, thinking perhaps it was another case of mistaken identity. "Dumb idiot," I thought later about myself. "Oh well."

We found the gay bar, also around the corner, and hit it often for dancing. It started late and was full of light shows and phony smoke from a fog machine. Not really my thing, but Tommy was also up for the salsa clubs, where I had the exquisite experience of being applauded for a cha-cha-cha. Well, they don't call him Doctor Dance for nothing. He also was up for an appearance at my danzón lesson with Laura. A new syntax for him, but one he quickly learned. Dancers have their own language, like railroaders comparing hand signals. I could tell danzón did not capture him. He was really all about the foxtrot.

Danzón was more of a woman's orgasm. Slow, restricted, with an explosive third act.

But I digress.

When we were leaving for our usual beach trip reward for the students, Tommy showed up at the crack of dawn in his shorts and with his gym bag, in spite of having closed the bar the night before. We had the usual awful bus trip to get there—not the dreamy train to Veracruz. He was a trooper. I found him an economy hotel across the square from ours in La Crucecita, the Mexican workers' town in the center of the posh Huatulco beach resort. Huatulco was no Acapulco, we found out. No gay bars, just family establishments. No matter. Tommy made friends with a boatman named Juan, and the four of us, Caroline, Tommy, Joanne, and I, rented his boat all day. I had brought my boom box and a mess of salsa records. The great Cuban salsa singer Celia Cruz had just died, so we memorialized her in and out of the bays of Huatulco, where Juan took us into every inlet. Now we had a soundtrack. Tommy sat in the bow, downing Tecates like a lord. Juan soon decided his masculinity required he pick up two maids at the hotels for insurance, so we became seven. At 2:00 p.m. Juan left us at a remote beach and went to pick up lunch. Tommy started giving salsa lessons to the maids. The day was floating, cha-cha-cha in the sand, Celia singing "Babalú." Later, we snorkeled and chased bright blue fish with electric-yellow spots. Tommy found a conch.

"There I was in the disco," Tommy said, "with purple bell bottoms and hair down to my ass, when a Fred Astaire Dance Studio scout spotted me. 'How'd you like to do this for a living?' And I moved to Atlanta. Finally had to cut my hair. I wouldn't cut it before. Not even when my old man bailed me out of jail on the condition that I cut it. Really pissed him off."

We stayed out way past the agreed-on time, cruising into Santa Cruz harbor to Celia's "Tu voz," all the mermaids snoozing, a Fellini finale, with Tommy in the bow, still the raconteur.

"We were at the nationals, and this student had a routine worked out with three female dancers. Well, one of them got sick, and so this male instructor had to fill in. I mean, they don't refund your money at that point. Anyway, we dressed him up, and in the finale, where the three women are doing a can-can number and flipping their dresses up in front of the judges, he flips his dress up, and he had tucked a big wig into his dance pants. I was sitting right behind the judges, and it was bush city. They were livid. He was fired on the spot."

We giggled helplessly.

"You think that one is funny. Let me tell you about the time I got locked out of my hotel in New Orleans on a four-day student trip."

"Stop, Tommy, stop," we said.

"Well, we went out to some gay bar on Bourbon Street, and all I had on was my shorts, a white T-shirt, some money, a room key, and my sneakers. We were leaving in the morning, so the other instructor went back to the hotel, but after I spent all my money, I went out with someone who took me to a big park with a locked iron gate.

"'Here's how you get in,' he said, stretching the chain open and sliding through. So there we were in the big park, and he says, 'You have a nice ass—take your shorts off and turn around.' So I did, and when I turned back around, he was gone with my shorts and my sneakers and my room key."

"Oh, Tommy," we said.

"Yes," he said, "all I had was my white BVD T-shirt. So I took it off and put my legs through the armholes and kind of tied it around the waist and squeezed back through the big iron gate. The sun was coming up, and people with briefcases were going to work. The students were having breakfast in the hotel, and I thought, 'They can't see this.' Of course, I didn't have my room key—so I had to explain myself to the desk clerk. 'I've been mugged,' I said. 'They stole all my clothes.' And he had to call the room and wake up my roommate, and when he saw me in the hall, he said, "Baity, I don't have time now, but later, I want to hear all the details.""

We docked with a little bump, us rolling from side to side laughing, Celia Cruz singing "Noche criolla." Juan promised to meet us later in town, after he had cleaned up the conch shell.

Caroline and Joanne were in collapse. Me, not so much—so later, when the sun went down, Tommy and I set out to make the clubs, starting with the cheap one on the square. Not too much dance space, but Tommy liked the bartender. He told us where to go at the resort end of town. Light-and-sound show. A line outside and the ubiquitous fog machine. We got out on the floor early and claimed enough space for a cha-cha-cha. More applause. Well, I had my moment, then Tommy and I sat, dishing the dancers. I felt like María Rojo at the café in Veracruz in the movie *Danzón*.

"Ha," he responded when I said something about the way a woman moved, "I get you. You like to watch. You are a voyeur."

"Writer, voyeur," I said, "what's the difference? You need the details."

"Go on, ask her," he urged. "You never know." I demurred. She wasn't there alone.

At midnight, with the bus trip back starting at 7:00 a.m. the next day, we called a cab. I asked Tommy if he wanted me to have the driver take him around the square to his hotel, but he said no, he'd rather walk.

"Good night," I said. "See you early." The tinny music from the overhead bar was still jangling in the streetlights.

I slept like the dead and in the morning herded the students onto the bus, sleepwalkers, spilling their snacks and water bottles. No Tommy. I walked across the square and rapped on his door.

"Just got here an hour ago—be up in a minute," he told me. "I was walking across the square when I heard music."

The next day I got the rest of the story. The amiable bartender was ready to go out when Tommy went back to our starting point, and they repeated the bar crawl. Serendipitously, the two maids were waiting in the line outside the light-and-sound disco, and Tommy and the bartender invited them in. Those cha-cha-cha lessons on the sand paid off, but Tommy told me that the bartender preferred to dance with him. So after dropping the girls off, they repaired to the park bench, which happened to be under the hotel window Caroline and I were dead to the world in, and, well, they were there until approximately an hour before I knocked on his door.

"Glad the students were sleeping it off, too," I thought. But then it would have been good for them, one student in particular. She had spent the trip gossiping about Caroline and me to the other students, one of whom was a lesbian who then felt silenced.

"Little poison pen," I thought. "Why can't a twenty-year-old just think about her own sex life? I would have."

The next year Joanne and I tried to recreate the boat trip with Juan, but nobody could tell us where he moored his boat, though of course they gave us directions anyway. We finally gave up trying to find him and just went inside the sterile hotel on the beach at Tangolunda, where Juan had picked up the waitresses for our ride, and had a lemonade. Without Tommy, the selkie mist was off the shore.

Vicente Hernández Vásquez, Virgin of Juquila, San Martín Tilcajete, Oaxaca, 2006. Wood, 8 × 4 × 2 in. Private collection.

CHAPTER TWENTY-ONE

El Pedimento de Amialtepec

Juquila, Oaxaca, December 2010

I WAS ON the coast of Oaxcaca in December to visit a place Pedro had been telling me about for years, the Pedimento de Amialtepec. He said this shrine, and the church in the nearby town of Santa Catarina Juquila, were the most important indigenous sites of pilgrimage in Oaxaca. Every year millions of people came, on foot, on bicycle, and in car and truck caravans, to ask the Virgin of Juquila, called affectionately Juquilita, for favors or to thank her.

A Spanish priest brought her statue, less than two feet tall, to Amialtepec in the sixteenth century, and eventually she was placed in a church, where she performed many miracles. A fire destroyed the church and the town, but her wooden image survived, although it was darkened, like the color of the indigenous people's skin. It was then that church authorities decided to move the image to a new church in the nearby town of Santa Catarina Juquila, but the Virgin would not stay there. Three times she escaped and returned to Amialtepec, hiding in a cave, drinking from a spring, and returning to her mountain, called El Pedimento. Eventually, she consented to remain in Santa Catarina Juquila.

The Pedimento now has a new chapel where there is a ceramic

copy of the statue of the Virgin, and the hill itself, being made of clay, is used by pilgrims to model figures of their requests, which they leave on the mountain.

I had hired a taxi in Puerto Escondido to come here, a journey of four hours, and the driver led me up the path to the chapel, cut-paper banners in joyous colors unfurling in the currents of air. I walked around the chapel to the mountainside itself, and I felt my breath stop and tears come to my eyes. There were storage buildings full of crosses, so high they reached the ceilings. The trees, shaking in the wind, had crosses tied to their branches. Unfurling like long hair, they clattered and moved. Other offerings dangled—a painted teacup, sneakers, flowers, paintings, rags, banners, arrows—but mostly crosses. Alive and shingling. All the trees all the way down the mountain were laden. Then I looked down. I was standing on art. Clay modeled figures returning to soil. The ground was covered with them. Requests of the Virgin.

The pilgrims had modeled the elements of their lives: a house, a garden, a pine tree, a pig, a family, a child, a quadrangle written upon, a *milagro*—a small charm—stuck while wet over a play-money 1,000-peso note. There was piped water for fashioning the clay, and I noticed a family, father in baseball cap, mother with long silver braids, making *figuras* to leave on the mountain. They had with them woven ixtle bags, water bottles, and rolled petate mats to sleep on. Watching them, I felt my life dissolving, being swept away. Without thinking, I asked for more good time for my friend Mary Grathwol, who was dying of cancer. Her sister later told me that Mary's last month was pain free, and she got up on the morning of her death looking for God.

A tape was playing a pilgrim's song. The *Misa*, or Mass, of the mountain.

The trail wound all the way down, but I didn't follow it that

day. A river of the people had been here five days before, for the
Virgin's feast day on December 8, and flowed up this mountain
and down the valley to Santa Catarina Juquila. The taxi driver and
I drove there next, and I went to the new church, where it was all
about crowd control; pews only for *ancianos* (old people) or com-
municants. Samsung flat-screens made announcements. Barriers
funneled us to the niches holding her old holy clothes. We could
walk near the altar, where many bins held *cartas*, letters for the
Virgin. Later we passed behind her mantle, only inches from her
long black hair. She rested upon an agave cactus.

The courtyard would have been full of sleepers on their mats
on her feast day. The whole medieval town, full of indigenous people, winding up streets, pilgrims waiting to come close.

So many border crossers take her image with them that she is
known as the Virgin of the Migrants.

Pedro and I did take the students to Juquila in the summer of
2011, but in Oaxaca City, beforehand, he took us to the alternate
destination for people who cannot make the pilgrimage, the
Church of San Juan Chapultepec. His mother used to take him
there. Up on the hill behind this church there was a natural cave,
which was another *pedimento*. On an altar inside the cave was a
replica of Juquilita, and pasted against the walls and on niches
carved into them were figuras and gifts of gratitude. Since the
Spanish often built churches on sites previously considered sacred,
the duality continued, with the official and the natural coexisting.
The Spanish allowed indigenous dances to take place outside the
church on fiesta days, another acceptance of coexistence.

I realized that there must be thousands of such enchanted
places, or *encantos*, in Mexico, such the Hill of Tepeyac, where the
Virgin of Guadalupe appeared to the Indian Juan Diego, and the
Cerro Quemado of the Wixárika. The following year Pedro took

us to yet another in Reyes Etla, just outside of Oaxaca City. The official Templo del Señor de las Peñas was a church built on top of an indigenous temple, whose unexcavated ruins still surrounded the site. Inside the church were statues of the Virgin of Guadalupe and of Juquilita. Outside was a rocky outcrop with an imprint of a human foot, known as the footprint of God when he sat and rested after having made the earth. This was a local pedimento heavily visited during the town's fiesta on the fifth Friday of Lent.

Being an unbeliever myself, I felt nevertheless the power of the sacred. I felt that this power was brought to the sites in the arms of the people and newly created each time in each place. It unified the mixed cultures of Mexico, energized the community, allowed visitors in and assimilated them, and enacted the collective will of the people. Here was the communal prayer that supported the migrant on his or her travels.

I understood how far ranging the Virgin of Juquila's worship was when I visited Chiapas in 2015. On San Lorenzo's Day, in August, I went with Helga, the director of the San Cristóbal language school Instituto Jovel, to Zinacantán. Driving in, we saw their plastic-roofed greenhouses checkering the green hills. I had seen their flowers in the Abastos Market in Oaxaca City and had been told they drove to Mexico City to the Sonora Market. Parking, we walked toward the center of town with other visitors, who were mostly from surrounding villages. We noticed the Maya couture, of course, but also the shiny, decked-out trucks with decals and titles named for Juquilita. The truckers, I have since learned, make pilgrimages to Santa Catarina Juquila to visit her.

The church at Zinacantán always felt welcoming to me and joyous. Today was no exception, with townspeople crowding in but with no disaffection for visitors. Musicians played harps and homemade guitars, and the guilds came in and out of the nave, enacting rituals in the magic time frame of the fiesta. We were lost in their musical time. Inside the church, in a side chapel, the Virgin of Juquila had her niche. Her altar was a wall of fresh-cut tuberoses, lilies of the valley, asters, and ginger flowers. She wore a long satin robe with lace and a macramé necklace with coins and ribbons. We asked about her presence.

"Oh, yes, she is here, but she has her own church in Navenchauc," a man told us. Navenchauc was the sister pueblo to Zinacantán.

The following year, Helga and I went there to see. The first church we got to as we came into the village was dedicated to her. A carved wooden sign over the door read: "*1994, Recuerdo para el Templo de Virgen de Juquila y Señor de Tila.*" An illuminated cross in the colors of the Republic stood on the roof, with the Virgin of Juquila depicted in neon. Inside, the nave was flanked by forty large vases of fresh-cut roses. A banquette of candles glowed in front of the altar. Three icons shared the altar: the Virgen de los Remedios; the Señor de Tila, a black Christ; and Juquilita, this time wearing a Zinacantecan cape, heavily embroidered. Someone had the three-year *cargo*, or charge, to change her clothing and flowers every fifteen days.

"Good to be a saint here," I thought. "Lots of perks."

A family who lived next door was busy trimming flowers on their porch. They were glad to tell us the history of her church. It turned out to revolve around the usual wars between the Mexican political parties, the National Action Party, the PAN, and the Institutional Revolutionary Party, the PRI.

"It was a political matter," the father said. "Then the PAN was fighting the PRI, and so the PAN built this church for their members. The PRI had built the other church in town for the Virgin of Guadalupe. Now everybody uses both of them."

"But there are pilgrimages to Juquila?" I asked.

"Yes," he said, "in December."

We went to the Virgin of Guadalupe's church in the town center, and there was a photographic image of Juquilita next to her on the altar. Of course, why the PAN picked Juquilita for Navenchauc is still a mystery. Did the locals meet her as the Virgin whose image was carried by migrants across the US border and within Mexico? Did they encounter her while selling flowers on their travels? A tourist guide I met told me that the Zinacantecans, being salesmen, were very politic and would include a neighboring state's Virgin as a goodwill gesture. The scholar John Burstein told me that they have been traders since Aztec times, this area having been an outpost for tribute. Their towns certainly felt inclusive in a way that other nearby towns did not.

Whatever the connection, Juquilita was at home here. Attributes she shared with El Señor de Tila were her dark skin color, her association with a cave and a mountain, and her reputation for miraculous healing.

Epifanio Fuentes, Mermaid, San Martín Tilcajete, Oaxaca, 1994.
Wood, 13 × 13.5 × 8 in. Private collection.

CHAPTER TWENTY-TWO

Land of the Sun

Oaxaca City, Christmas 2013

TWENTY-TWO YEARS AFTER I first saw Oaxaca, I was waiting for the bus at El Llano Park. The bus arrived, and it was blue and named for Juquilita, the little Virgin of Juquila. I now noticed her everywhere. We were going to the Abastos Market, eight square blocks, its location next to the second-class bus station, an arrangement for people bringing livestock, produce, and everything else to the city. Six pesos' fare—I grabbed the rail to get on. Inside, everyone was wearing couture jeans, since they are made in Mexico. Juquila's tin retablo, or votive painting, in the middle of the windshield next to a leather quirt. And Jesus on the cross. As we bounced on down the block, I thought about how every day is different in the Mesoamerican calendar, how it fosters acceptance. I got off when the woman next to me did, on the periphery of the market. I like the periphery best—it's the most innovative and eclectic part.

Socks, Christmas lights blinking, Calvin Klein briefs, flashing electric candy canes, knapsacks, baseball caps, aroma of copal. Sharp smell of roasted chile pork; plastic Barbie Jeeps pink and purple with decals; sandals; tropical fruit, mamey and watermelon;

cucumber; tlayudas; *jamoncillo* from the town of Juquila. Bread, mittens, ski hats, magnets, turtles, lilies, fireworks, baby Crocs, tangerines, thongs, leather belts, a nonfunctioning lottery machine, pickled *ciruelas*, a man with a very high-tech video camera, moving like a ninja. In a basket: tomatillos, potatoes, onions, string beans, limes. A drugstore Santa, a candy store clown, a man wearing a white "Sánchez Family Peregrination Juquila November 2012" T-shirt, skull ski masks costing 120 pesos—I was tempted—and, in the boutique section, luggage, embroidered shirts for musical groups, a woman passing with a basket of bright red radishes on her head, a gray apron over her red skirt, long gray braids, and red ribbon. Movies, tacos, dried fish, candy, underpants, long-distance phone calls, botanica, items for magic, copal, statues of Santa Muerte, Ganesh, and El Indio, dried sea urchins, medicinal plants, grasshoppers, manicures, piñatas, prom dresses, oilcloth, pet food, a basket of onions, turkeys, *cal*, machetes, a flower lady in blue with blue-ribboned braids.

I needed to eat. At twelve thirty I sat down just anywhere at the first *comedor*, and I was at Nieves Juquilita, having a *manzana* soda and a zapote negro snow cone. The booth was surrounded by pink flashing mini-lights, icicle style, six silver and fuchsia shell Christmas ornaments, a small television ornamented with two pink butterflies, and, covering a shelf in the rear, a fine rebozo from Xochistlahuaca in cream with pink, green, orange, and yellow brocade. A Juquila tin altar, also pink, hung on the back wall. They sold snow cones of prickly pear fruit, *limón*, *melón*, mango, zapote, guayaba, tamarindo, guanabana, *nuez*, coco, *fresa*, mescal, mamey, sorbet, *leche quemada*, and *pétalos de rosa*. Other families were eating lunch, a beautiful Zapotec woman with five sons, wearing a pink rebozo around her head, which she let fall as she warmed up. The couple next to me brought their own tortillas and roasted onions for the restaurant to heat up, and they purchased watermelon water to go with it. Rested, I continued on. Red brassieres and panties for pregnancy in the New Year, cell phones, pornography.

I took the bus back home, this time named Guadalupe, inside a red zone, *"Compárame,"* Compare Me, as the driver's slogan, two red lights, a buxom angel, Jesus on the ceiling with a red dingleberry frame, Guadalupe inside over the windshield in a tin frame, names of his children, Alexander, Alejandra, Ferro, the slogan *"Amantes escondidos,"* Hidden Loves, a red furry mirror frame, fur dice, a red eight-ball wheel knob, a Guadalupe shift changer, the seat wound in green elastic cord, the CD player with norteño music playing, a red velvet curtain over the windshield with gold tassels, red fur-framed side mirrors, a child's sandal attached to the grip rods, a pink woven change basket, a yellow plastic bucket filled with soapy water and a rag.

I got off at El Llano Park and headed for Xiguela, where I ate the best sandwich in Oaxaca, smoked trout with arugula, shaved carrot, and tomato on ciabatta. A jar of mango water. A blue Juquilita morning returned by a red Virgin of Guadalupe. Later I met a conch-playing Maya day keeper, or astrologer, who told me, "Talk to the stars, and then you won't need a psychologist."

Oaxaca City, June 2014

When I first saw the Pedroarona family tomb, I thought it looked like a cheap motel room on the Day of the Dead—concrete with a frosted-glass sliding door, vases inside with dead flowers. This is why I had no trouble finding the grave today, more than twenty years later. I was looking for Elda, my phone call to her house having brought me the news of her death, two weeks too late to see her.

My taxi on the way over reeked of gas, but the driver played loud jazz on his radio—"Mambo No. 5" and Cole Porter. I appreciated the contrast with my grief. A breezy day, an old man sweeping, a young woman offering to help me find my way. But the grave was right where it was in the memory of that day. I had two bunches of plastic flowers with me, purple and red. Elda was not here, only Lupita, name inscribed in marble stone, and the grandson, who died so young. The flowers inside were dry. I wedged mine into the door.

"I'm writing about you," I said. "And I'm gay. Sorry I did not trust you enough to tell you before."

I didn't think Elda was there, so I asked in the office, was her name in the book? The man on duty leafed through what looked like a school composition book with inked-in names of the dead. They directed me to the administration office back in town.

The taxi driver consoled me. "Your Spanish is very good."

"I learned it from them," I said.

"Yes," he said, "but to this house we all must come. My father, dead thirty-one years, and it was yesterday."

He held me in a net of words. I gave him exact change, left with a blessing.

Elda was not in the computer either, at the administration office, so they directed me to the funeral home, but I chose to get off the path and stopped in the church we had gone to on Christmas three years before, after her nephew had died and where we heard the chorus. She fell asleep during the music. Hard times, those years after Lupita died, when Elda's sisters wanted the house and were ignoring her.

"We were like two little old ladies," she said about Lupita.

Of course Lupita left her the house, but now with the real estate bubble, it had value. She went to Huatulco with the maid, and she enjoyed singing boleros with me, particularly when I showed her how to use YouTube—she told me God had sent me to show her how to use it, but I could see how the deaths and the jealousy were hurting her.

"It's a clash of old and new," I told Pedro. "She followed the custom her whole life, but now real estate comes in."

"How could she move at seventy?" Pedro said. "People don't do that."

Well, now she has, sinvergüenza sisters.

Coming out of the church, I found I was in front of the funeral home after all, and after asking for her here, I found out that she died at 6:00 p.m. on May 30 and her ashes were not in the *panteón* but in the rear wall of Santo Domingo in a niche. Her post office box in the wall read "Fam. Gonzales Pisano." Her given name did not appear.

Elda, la güera, always knew where she came from and where she was going. She didn't travel. Lupita went once to Spain, the family story told over and over, how hard it was to have the mother leave, her only voyage. They didn't have many students in the house. It was too hard to have them become friends and leave, myself, Barbara, the dancing man. Elda was not born on García Vigil, but in another mansion on Porfirio Díaz Street. It was a family scandal when a relative turned it into a disco.

"Elda was of the upper class here," Lizbeth told me. "It is expensive to have your ashes in Santo Domingo."

To that house, we do not all come.

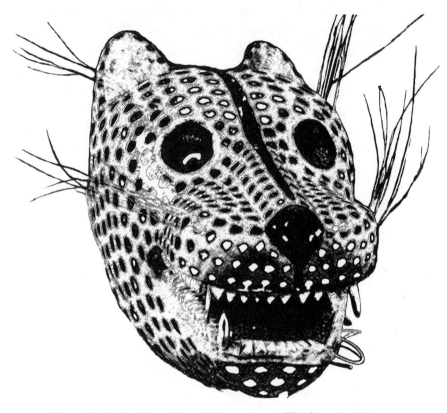

Jaguar Mask, Guadalupe Victoria, Guerrero, 1992. Wood, 14 × 8 × 8 in. Private collection.

CHAPTER TWENTY-THREE

Welcome Home, Son of Pakal

San Cristóbal de las Casas, July, 2015

I MET RUBÉN while he was standing in the atrium of the Teatro Daniel Zebadúa in San Cristóbal de las Casas. I wanted to talk to him, but he was working, enticing spectators to buy tickets to *Pakal, Heart of Jade*, a play by the theater company Palenque Rojo. A beautiful man with waist-length black hair, olive eyes, and the body of a dancer, he was wearing a cape of jade and quetzal feathers, a draped leather loincloth, jade wristlets, jade breast ornaments, and a headdress of a feathered green macaw with open beak, and he was holding an ornate obsidian spear. When he found an empty moment, he agreed to tell me the story of his border crossing.

Rubén grew up under the volcanos Popocatépetl and Iztaccíhuatl, his *municipio* of Ixtapaluca divided by the *cuota* highway to Puebla. The main city is at 9,000 feet, with scattered pueblos up to 12,792 feet. It is considered a suburb of Mexico City, and it has a few factories, but most workers commute into the Distrito Federal. Last year it was one of the worst cities in Mexico for femicides. Leaving was a reasonable choice for a good future. But his reason for leaving was different.

At eighteen he had a good life unfolding, a girlfriend he was in business with, tattooing and body piercing, but she had problems. She was bipolar and succeeded in killing herself. Rubén felt like he had lost everything. He started to travel aimlessly, not looking to kill himself, but perhaps to find someone who would kill him. He was fighting a lot in the streets, but nobody could hurt him. Finally, Julio, his older brother, said, "Why don't you go to the States and find our father? Maybe things will change for you there." His journey was really to lose himself, the person he couldn't stand to be anymore. He crossed the border in 2006, looking to forget.

"We crossed from Nogales, Sonora, and walked nine hours in the mountains until we got to a safe house," he told me. "We were all in good shape—two military men, a man into sports, and I was used to climbing in the mountains. Mountains were nothing to me. We were to wait there to be picked up. We were crouched down in a ditch. They told us, 'Don't stand up, or people might shoot you in the head.' We could hear a noise like the wind getting louder and louder, and then there were airplanes overhead, the Border Patrol. We got picked up in a truck by the coyotes and taken to Phoenix and then Tucson. The first place I worked was Las Vegas. A lot of *salvadoreños* I worked with rode the train to the border, and they told stories of people losing their lives or parts of their bodies. Their parents sent them, saying, 'I would rather think of you dead on the road seeking a good future than to die in the street in El Salvador from the gangs.'"

I thought about the border I had seen from the trains while working out of Tucson and El Paso. We would see migrants, looking so young, taking shelter from the sun under railroad cars on some siding in the middle of nowhere. Even the rednecks would not deny them water. We knew how deadly hot it was.

"After three weeks in Las Vegas, I worked in Louisiana for two years, cleaning up after Katrina, rebuilding houses, but first pulling dead people out of houses. I worked for a contractor, and the sheriff, a Korean guy, was racist toward black people but not toward Mexicans. He would take black people to jail but just tell us, 'You're OK. You don't get into trouble—you do your work.' Pulling out dead bodies was unpleasant, but it didn't really bother me that much. I'm from Mexico City, and I had seen a lot of dead bodies. Walking to school, you would see dead bodies. After weekend parties, there would be bodies. So, other than the smell, cleaning up after Katrina didn't scare me. I saw a lot that changed my thinking about the United States, though. People were sleeping outside on the streets rather than go into shelters. The police wouldn't do anything if someone was attacked, robbed, or raped in a shelter. They would say, 'We are too few against the many.' They would just stay outside.

"In 2010 the construction company sent me to fix the roof of that sheriff Joe Arpaio in Maricopa County, Arizona. There was a big hailstorm, and his roof was damaged. We thought it was funny because he was so racist against Mexicans, but the boss said not to say anything."

Joe Arapio said, "Ours is an operation where we want to go after illegals. It's a pure program. You go after them, and you lock them up." After they fix your roof.

"I stayed the longest in Oklahoma City. There I began to play the bass and found myself as a musician. I worked construction to earn money, but as soon as work was over I was making music. I like heavy metal. It's unusual to find Mexicans who like heavy metal. I was in the mosh pit with the American people. One time this really big guy came at me, and I did my moves and threw him off me. I didn't know what would happen, because he was in the

New York Death Militia, one of their big guys. But he came up and hugged me, and some people said, 'Now you are all right if he says you are.' We called our band Kick Flip, from the skateboard move, but people said it sounded too much like happy punk, and I didn't want to be happy. Then our drummer went to jail for a year, and we waited for him, but when he got out, he left town chasing his girlfriend, so we got a new drummer and a new name, Psychopaths.

"There was an audience for Mexican heavy metal. There were two Mexican bands, us and Overdose, but they were Mexicans from California. We used to put on these fiestas in the neighborhood, no cover, free beer, and lots of people came and liked our music, so we made demos and took them down to the Conservatory. Lots of big-name bands played there, so we were kind of nervous showing our demo, but they had already heard about us from the fiestas, and they said, 'Sure, you can play, you can open for some bands.' The biggest band we opened for was D.R.I. That was incredible, playing on the same stage with D.R.I.

"I also had a girlfriend, and we had a daughter together. We were happy, but there were problems. I wanted us to marry, and she was afraid I only wanted a Green Card. She listened to her friends who told her things like that. But we had a daughter, so it was more than the Green Card. She tried to keep me from seeing my daughter, so we ended up in family court. She charged things against me—that I was on drugs; that I sold drugs—but the court found me clean, so I got to see my daughter. The judge asked me what I wanted, and I said, 'I want to see my daughter, and I want to pay child support.'"

Rubén told me his young daughter, along with his ex-girlfriend, was coming to visit him in Chiapas. I could imagine her delight to see him in the production as the prince of Palenque. I couldn't help feeling the border—the shadow border this time—was again in play in his relationship. I could tell there were two things he really cared about in the United States: his daughter and his music.

"After a while, I started to want to do more with my instrument, to learn more, and so I moved to Dallas," he said. "There I teamed up with a guitar player named Martirio, who played porn gore–style music, splatter death metal. We found a drummer, Flaco, who used to play with Ritual de Brujas, but they broke up, and we three rented a studio and developed five songs. I knew we needed about thirteen. In Dallas we were involved with a group called Akelarre, who did dance performance art. It used the folklore of witchcraft. I am very interested in folklore.

"So there I was in Dallas, with my band and my fiancée and daughter in Oklahoma City, and lots of work, and then Julio, my brother, who I hadn't seen in nine years, went on vacation to the United States. He was in Philadelphia with his girlfriend, and he told her, 'I have to go see my brother.' So he came to Dallas, and he saw everything I had, and he really appreciated it, and he recognized that I was doing good things, but he saw that everything was not so good in my heart, and he said, 'Brother, come home with me to Mexico. We are doing interesting things in Chiapas, and you can join us.'

"And what I felt—I just felt an opening in my heart, like I had just been waiting for nine years for someone to find me and say, 'Come home,' and I knew I had to go home with him. My fiancée didn't understand why I could leave everything. I told her she could come to Mexico, too. She was Hispanic and spoke Spanish, but she didn't want to leave the US. So I worked for a week, and with that money, we took a bus to the border. I just took my guitar and a backpack.

"When we crossed the bridge, the Mexican *migra* asked me, 'Do you have an ID?'

"I said, 'No.'

"He said, 'Are you Mexican?'

"I said, 'Yes.'

"He said, 'Why do you want to come back?'

"I said, 'I'm tired.'

"He said, 'Welcome to Mexico.'

"As soon as I crossed, what I felt was freedom.

"When we got to Mexico City, my brother said, 'What do you want? You can do anything you want.'

"I said, 'I want to drink pulque!' So we went drinking pulque, and afterwards we went to my mother's house, and I stayed in the shadows. She came to the door and said, 'Julio, you only come to see me when you are drunk.' And he said, 'Do you want me to go away then?' And he brought me out of the shadows, and she saw me there for the first time in nine years. We ate a lot of good cooking at her house.

"When I went outside, the streets were empty. I remembered them being full of my friends, people in the neighborhood gangs. But now there were only some kids on the corners, and they asked me, 'What drugs do you want?'

"I said, 'No, I'm back. I'm from here.' And I saw a big guy with a big gun keeping an eye on them.

"When they learned who I was, they said, 'You're a legend. We heard about you fighting all these guys. We're meeting a legend.'

"I went to find Benny, a friend of mine, and I saw him on another street, so I came up behind him and said, '*Chinga tu madre,*' and he ran off down the street scared and jumped into a house, and I followed him and saw him inside the house with a crack pipe, and he recognized me finally, but catching up I found out a lot of my friends were dead or in jail or strung out. A few of us got together again and peopled the streets for a few days, but I didn't want to stay in that neighborhood. So I went to Chiapas with my brother."

Julio was the brother who had discovered San Cristóbal de las Casas and found work first in the theater. I asked him what he had found when he went to see Rubén in Dallas. "Was he OK?"

"He was working framing houses, so he was strong, but he didn't look good," Julio said. "His face was all sunburned, he had lost a front tooth, and he had sad eyes. He was sleeping on an inflatable mattress in the living room of some other workers. He had his music, but he wasn't OK. The work was awful. They were building mansions for *pinche gringos ricos*, fucking rich white people, and getting paid badly, *pago de madre*. All for the illusion of dollars. The workers were losing their identity and their *espíritu*, their spirituality.

"We had lunch with Rubén's boss, and we told him we were going back home. His face totally changed. He spent the hour telling us his money troubles, how he had to pay for everything and how he wasn't making anything either."

"Did Rubén save anything during his time in the United States?"

"No, because he was young and partying and in the music scene and moving around to follow the work. We took the bus to the border because Rubén didn't have papers. When we got there, the Mexican migra asked for his papers, and he didn't have them.

"'Did you commit a crime in the US?' the migra asked him. 'Is that why you are leaving?'

"'No.'

"'Why, then?'

"'*Mi vida esta acá*.' My life is here.

"'*Bienvenido, paisano.*' Welcome home, countryman."

Julio had found the acting job in Chiapas, where his two broth-ers now work with him. I asked him how he wound up there. He left home even earlier than Rubén, at the age of fifteen, but he went to the Distrito Federal, Mexico City. Rubén was thirteen when his brother left home.

"I was enjoying the city, living in the Lagunilla area, hanging out in pulquerias, where for a few pesos you can have food: beans, cheese, and tortillas. I met an older woman, Carina, who was from the DF, who knew how to get along in the Lagunilla, selling used clothes from the US for a big profit in all the flea markets. I would buy a pair of pants for 5 pesos and sell them for 200. I specialized in military uniforms. We also did street theater in the Metro, playing pre-Hispanic instruments. She was very street smart, *muy cabrona*, but she was always very jealous and dramatic, and she broke my heart. The first one is the worst.

"I went back home, depressed, but I had a friend, Bruno, who rescued me. His father bought Café la Selva in the Cineteca Nacional in the DF, and he invited me to work there. It was a great place to be working because everyone came through there, musi-cians, students, directors, actors. My friend was studying at UNAM [Universidad Nacional Autónoma de México] with Julio Estrada, the ethnomusicologist, and we got to work on a music project with him. Of course, I went back to my crazy cabrona girlfriend again. Bruno couldn't believe it. She wanted me to go traveling, to Cancún, to southern Mexico, and she was friends with the woman Isabel who owned Restaurante Madre Tierra in San Cristóbal. Isabel liked to come to the DF to see the *lucha libre*, the Mexican wrestling, and I met her. When we were going to travel to Cancún and Tulum, we also went to San Cristóbal and stayed for a while. We were looking forward to hearing this

DF band play there, Antidoping. The strangest thing happened. We were staying in this hostel called Casa Azul, and they were having a party. I had my drums, and outside I met some musicians with their drums, and we all went inside together, and everyone thought we were all together in the same band, and so we played together—and the musicians were Antidoping, the band that we went to San Cristóbal to see. I was eighteen years old then. Anyway, they told me to go to Cuba to learn percussion, so that's where I got the idea.

"Back in the DF I got a *beca*, a scholarship, to study in Cuba— actually the beca was to study medicine, because they wouldn't give me a beca to study music, but I really wanted to study percussion. I went to Cuba, but it didn't work out for me. This woman asked me to carry something for her, and it turned out to be contraband, and the customs agent made me return. So I lost my dream, and it made me really sad. But I liked San Cristóbal, and so I returned there and got a job working as a bouncer in the Madre Tierra and selling things on the side. My girlfriend, Carina, was there too, and life got out of hand partying. It really was an *inframundo*, an underworld, there at Madre Tierra because it stayed open all night until 10:00 a.m.

"I was working the street, handing out flyers for the Madre Tierra, and I met the theater people from Palenque Rojo handing out their flyers. I was really interested in their pre-Hispanic music, and I volunteered to work for no money just to play drums with them. After a while they asked me to join them because one of the older actors broke his kneecap."

"Break a leg!" I said.

"Yes, he broke his leg. Oh, and my girlfriend ran off with an Italian. So for the first two months I was studying at the theater, history, music, literature. I met another woman, Adriana, a psychologist. I met her at the Madre Tierra. She was very smart and getting a PhD in Baltimore. So life was better.

"After a while I went to the DF to see my younger brother, Carlos, who was a painter. He was living with a woman who worked as a prostitute, and when he began to paint nudes, she offered the place where the women worked in the historical center as his studio. He could be the bouncer and paint all the women he wanted. Some hookers work from 8:00 a.m. to noon—we call them *mañaneras*, where businessmen go in the mornings. After 2:00 p.m. it was empty, and Carlos had it to himself. But one day some robbers with guns showed up and cleaned everybody out. Carlos got very depressed and went home to Ixtapaluca and just stayed in the house, drinking.

"I found him there and said, 'Why not come to San Cristóbal? You can probably get on in the theater, and you can drink there as well as here, but with more interesting people.' So he came with me. Before we left, his girlfriend invited us to her mother's house. Her father was dead, but he used to play the drum in a folkloric group called Danzantes del Sol. His big drum was in the house, and I started playing it. His mother came in the room and started to cry. I apologized, but she said, 'Take the drum, I prefer to have it beating than to have it here making me sad.' So I took my brother and the drum to San Cristóbal. This is the big drum we use in the production by Palenque Rojo."

Carlos is now playing the younger son of Pakal in the production.

As part of the cast, Julio got a visa—good for ten years—to tour with the play in Asheville, North Carolina, and Miami, Florida. He was able to use his visa a year later to go see his father in Miami, who had been working there with an uncle for many years. He couldn't go to see Rubén on that trip, but a year after that he went to see his new girlfriend, Jenny, in Philadelphia. Before he returned to Mexico, he went to Dallas to see Rubén, and that's when they came home together.

I attended the play the brothers acted in, *Pakal, Heart of Jade.* It is a dance spectacular designed for the tourist on the Ruta Maya who wants to see the archaeological sites they have just visited brought to life. In this it succeeds. The play is in Tzotzil Mayan, with English and Spanish subtitles projected on scrims. Roughly, the plot is that the end of a *katún*, or epoch, is upon Pakal, the ruler of Palenque. The next katún is one of death and warfare, and Pakal wishes to accept his fate and go down to Xibalba, the land of death. His son, Kan Balam II, played by Rubén, resists fate, and a drama plays out around this conflict. Pakal's three sons are in the forest hunting when Kan Balam kills a jaguar. His younger brother, played by Carlos, goes to retrieve it and is captured by Lord Po, prince of Toniná, a rival city. Kan Balam offers to settle the dispute royally by challenging Lord Po, played by Julio, to a ball game. The ball game, the game of life and death, and the story of humans' relationship to the gods symbolically stands for the fate of Pakal. If his sons win, then they have resisted the power of fate.

The ball game played by Lord Po and another warrior against the younger sons of Pakal is a choreographic delight. The walls of the theater become the ball court, and the scrim in front of the stage allows the ball to be an orb of light, like its cosmic reference. The players achieve a tie, but in the final match, the ball appears to have a course of its own, and fate scores the decisive goal. The two younger sons of Pakal resist the victory, but Pakal prevents them from violating the rules. He acknowledges their victory, and Kan Balam delivers the jaguar as tribute.

The finale of the play is the death of Pakal, the special effects showing him falling into the Milky Way of stars, ending with the image of his sarcophagus from Palenque.

I thought about Rubén's immersion in heavy metal folklore and Julio's pursuit of pre-Hispanic music, and I thought it wonderful that their work is now to enact some of the oldest folklore, but from their own country. Rubén's character challenges destiny, as he himself did by leaving for the States. Immigration is perhaps the new ball game, a game of life and death and destiny. According to Rubén, "When I came home, I felt complete. It is a big loss to lose your Mexican-ness, to not be able to feel your culture. Mexican people on the other side sometimes lose everything, even though they have work and new families sometimes. If someone dies in Mexico, they can lose everything, because they think, 'Why go home to see a box? I didn't see him when he was alive.' People change so much with the years. If I don't see my daughter for only a year, she will have changed a lot. You lose your family.

"Here in San Cristóbal, I think it is a little capital of the world. You meet people who are interested in the same things, and art is everywhere. Everywhere I look, I see art. It is here. It is there. I think San Cristóbal is the best place to love somebody. I have love for my work, I love to create, I love my daughter, I love myself, I love life, and I am complete. I love it that I make art with my body—like the Asians say, with the stomach, like the French say, with my liver, like Mexicans say, with my heart. It feels good to be in Mexico."

I was staying in Marcey and Janet's old house in San Cristóbal, and when I arrived, their aged gardener, Mateo, still working there, took both my hands in his and greeted me, "And how are you feeling in your heart?"

Glossary of Spanish Words and Phrases

alebrijes: Oaxacan, hand-painted wooden carvings of people, devils, and fantastical animals. (The papier-mâché originals were by Pedro Linares López in Mexico City.)

arracele: Rayon thread used in robozos.

artesanías: Crafts, folk art.

bordados huicholes: Huichol embroidery.

botánicas: Stores that sell medicinal herbs and magical items.

camisa: Man's shirt.

carrizo: Reed used in furniture making.

coleccionista: Collector.

coyuchi: Naturally brown cotton cloth or thread.

danzonera: Danzón orchestra; also used for a danzón dance group.

danzoneros: Danzón dancers.

day keeper: Among the Maya, the day keepers functioned as astrologers to interpret the nature of the days based on the Maya calendar. See also *Mesoamerican calendar*.

Dios espinoso: Spirit of the ceiba tree.

ex-votos: Paintings on metal or wood made with the purpose of thanking a saint.

Father Hidalgo: Father Miguel Hidalgo raised a banner of the Virgin of Guadalupe during his cry for Mexican independence in 1810.

fayuca: Untaxed goods sold on the street.

figuras: Figures.

fototeca: Photography archive.

gringa, gringo: A pejorative term for a foreign woman or man.

guaje: Tree native to Oaxaca with edible seeds.

guayabera: Man's shirt worn in Yucatán and Cuba.

guelaguetza: Oaxacan folk dance festival.

güera, güero: White or light-skinned woman or man.

huaraches: Leather sandals.

huipil: Indigenous woman's garment.

indigenismo: The glorification of indigenous cultures.

ixtle: Fibers made from the yucca and lechuguilla species of agave.

jerkail: Man's white wool serape from Chamula, Chiapas. It is woven from long fiber and combed out to have a nap.

jícara: Gourd.

La Llorona: In folk tales, a mother spirit who is heard crying for her children.

lechuguilla: Literally, "little lettuce," a type of agave plant.

limpia: A ritual cleansing.

Mantle of the Virgin of Guadalupe: The cloak belonging to the peasant Juan Diego, bearing a miraculous image of the Virgin. The image convinced Catholic Church authorities to believe Juan Diego's story that the Virgin had appeared to him.

maquiladora: Border factory owned by a US company where parts are assembled for import to the United States.

maquinista: Train engineer.

menesis: Grapevine step in danzón.

Mesoamerican calendar: The Mesoamerican calendar refers to similar systems of telling time among the major cultures of Mesoamerica. Basically there were two calendars, one a solar calendar of 365 days and the other a ritual calendar of 260 days.

The days were represented by drawings or glyphs. Each day had a distinct character, derived from the ruling glyph.

mestizaje: Mixed race.

metate: Flat pounding stone for making bark paper; grinding stone.

migrantes: Migrants.

nagual: Companion spirit animal.

PAN: Partido Acción Nacional, or National Action Party.

pan de muerto: Bread baked in human shapes for the Day of the Dead.

peines: Hair combs.

pedimento: A place of request, where people ask God or a saint for help.

petates: Straw mats.

PRI: Partido de la Revolución Mexicana, or Party of the Mexican Revolution.

quechquemitl: Pre-Hispanic triangular garment.

rebozo: Long, narrow shawl with distinctive crochet fringe.

remate: A shortened ending to a section of danzón music.

ropa: Clothes.

Ruta Maya: The tourist route to see Maya ruins; a bar crawl in San Cristóbal de las Casas.

Santa Rosa: Code for "marijuana."

separadores: Bookmarks.

tablas: Wooden tables for laying out bark paper to dry and shape.

traje: Traditional indigenous dress.

UNAM: Universidad Nacional Autónoma de México, or National Autonomous University of Mexico.

viloria: Reverse figure-eight step in danzón.

zócalo: The main square in a city.